I0021650

A PRACTICAL GUIDE TO PROTECTING YOUR ORGANIZATION AGAINST CYBERCRIME

MARK SANGSTER

CYBER CONSCIOUS LEADERSHIP

PAGE TWO

Cataloguing in publication information
is available from Library and Archives Canada.
ISBN 978-1-77458-552-8 (paperback)
ISBN 978-1-77458-553-5 (ebook)

Page Two
pagetwo.com

Cover and interior design by Fiona Lee

mbsangster.com

CONTENTS

A NOTE FROM THE AUTHOR

LIKE MOST THINGS in life, my career has refused to follow a linear trajectory and careened in directions I could never have predicted or imagined. Perhaps one of the greatest twists has been meeting the amazing people I have encountered along the way. As my wife is fond of saying, "People show you more of or less of what you want to be." In my case, colleagues and friends showed me a potential I would have otherwise missed.

For example, taking the stage with a genuine hero who flew in combat and chauffeured US presidents in Marine One was humbling on one hand and mind-blowing on another, as he deferred to me as the expert. My experience seemed minuscule in comparison to that of this man. It's a matter of perspective, I guess. And perhaps it's a matter of timing. Those you need come into your life when you need them.

In our own way, we each carry a lesson from which others can learn.

For this reason, I wanted to tell this story through the words of those who lived it. Each person brings a unique perspective that weaves a tapestry of hard-fought lessons. Their words are a proxy for their mistakes and successes and the emotional mileage they covered. By listening to their stories, we have the opportunity to shortcut our progress and do so without the same wear on our proverbial shoes.

Across the experts and practitioners I interviewed for this book, one common element stood out: they all bring a self-aware and curated approach to risk assessment and crisis decision-making. They are conscious of their choices rather than reacting to simplistic stimuli. They do not rush to action; they observe, orient, decide, and then act. In military parlance, it's known as the OODA loop, and it's a mental model that describes decision-making processes in highly stressful and chaotic environments like combat. Or a full-on cyberattack.

In essence, these experts are crisis-conscious. And that's the point of this book: to help business leaders and senior technical practitioners of cybersecurity become "cyber-conscious"—aware of one's cyber surroundings, acknowledging how one's inward state is driven by outward facts during cyber scenarios. Whether it's budgeting, planning, or responding to a business-disrupting crisis, being cyber-conscious means considering factors and risk in terms of business context, so that you can make informed and timely decisions that are not driven by emotional accelerants.

Creating a cyber-conscious culture takes awareness and a willingness to understand your enemy, determine your obligations, and hear things you don't want to hear. You might have to swallow the unpalatable. Regardless of the messenger or the implications of their message, cyber-conscious decision-making aims to understand the environment and then dilute the chaos and ambiguity with clear and unambiguous leadership through all cycles of cyber risk and response.

We all have a role to play in a cyber-conscious organization. Leaders must understand the expectations of their people. Employees must understand their roles and the decision-making lattice. Together they form a symbiotic OODA loop designed to mitigate risk and meet crisis head-on.

INTRODUCTION

DATA—OR THE information it contains—is the new currency. We are addicted to data. We believe data can and will solve business problems, ease public service issues, and make us more money. We collect and use client and customer data; human resource data; market, health, and education data; and more. Organizations rely on data for absolutely everything to connect people, services, and critical infrastructure. With the rise of AI, we chase new ways of using data that can create unlimited possibilities for advancing our business strategies. Data is the means and the end.

And yet, the more we rely on data, the more vulnerable we are.

Let's look, for example, at the data breach at 23andMe, the genome sequencing company that, for a fee and a quick saliva sample, reveals the secrets of consumers' genetic and family histories. On the surface, the company promises to protect its customers from potential harm, but they, arguably, are treading a thin line. In 2022, an in-depth assessment of its practices by *Consumer Reports* suggested that it was only a matter of time before 23andMe started selling its data to third parties, and by 2023 that was a reality.[1] Not only does every exchange of data present the potential for discrimination, even with articles of law such as the Genetic Information Nondiscrimination Act in the United States under effect. There is also an inherent risk of employers and insurance companies one day requiring genetic testing of their applicants in order to save money.

But that's not the worst risk associated with genome sequencing companies. By October 2023, 23andMe and its partner firms, DNA Relatives and Family Tree, experienced a massive data breach, exposing the genetic records of 6.9 million customers through a very simple account hack. That's why the UK Information Commissioner's Office and the Office of the Privacy Commissioner of Canada launched a joint investigation into 23andMe in June 2024.[2]

The risk, as it is plain to see, has folded over and wrapped around itself like the helical strands of DNA that 23andMe collects every day. We can no longer differentiate between what data we should collect and why. We can no longer anticipate risks as fully as is required. And we cannot protect our organizations, well meaning and ethical or not, from sending all of our unarmed and untrained stakeholders out onto the battlefield with us.

Behind the scenes of every organization, a war is being waged, and every one of us is on the firing line.

With every click, query, or online purchase, someone is watching and waiting to infiltrate our systems. The enemy has grown beyond unsophisticated smash-and-grab crimes; they're interested in *Ocean's Eleven*–style attacks that cripple our businesses, circumvent critical services like power generation and health care, erode our criminal justice systems and economies, and fuel distrust in our governments.

That's why it's important to understand that cyberattacks such as ransomware are no longer a string of isolated attacks. Cybercriminals and their nation-state sponsors have declared a silent war. Every day, we read about attacks that make up

Behind the scenes of every organization, a war is being waged, and we are on the firing line.

campaigns built on coordinated skirmishes that leave our lives on the front lines. We are at war.

Ransomware attacks are coordinated and connected to international political aims, and they are the main tactic in the cybercrime arsenal. It's no longer a question of whether you can protect your organization from a cyberattack but when you'll be forced to move into the fray. Ransomware is crowdsourced warfare with global consequences. All organizations are on the front lines.

The most glaring problem? No one is coming to save you but you. Because ransomware attacks are now ubiquitous, the current justice system and legal protections cannot stem the tide. A recent report from the US Government Accountability Office shows federal law enforcement agencies are ill prepared to combat the growing volume and ferocity of these cyberattacks.[3]

THAT'S WHY ransomware is no longer a technical issue, or even a business problem. It's a leadership dilemma. It requires cyber-conscious leadership that delivers accountability to investors, employees, partners, consumers, constituents, and the economy.

No matter the industry sector, leaders are responsible for taking bolder steps toward protecting their organizational interests. In this book, I'm going to share five essential tactics for leaders to implement right now to protect their organizations, and themselves, against digital invasions. It's about fostering a culture of cyber-consciousness. Drawing from critical advice offered up by my colleagues in cybersecurity, business leaders who faced ransomware attacks, and military intelligence, these tactics for shielding an organization from the enemy are tried, tested, and bulletproof.

In Part 1, I will illustrate the new world of cybersecurity and how it has become mapped to global warfare. In Part 2,

I'll investigate the baseline tactics you can use to ensure you have the right defensive framework in place. In Part 3, I'll offer five essential tactics for you to implement right now to protect against digital invasion, demonstrating exactly what is required to shield an organization from the enemy. Finally, Part 4 will bring your awareness to the future of cybercrime and what you can expect to face as this security threat evolves.

You can face the future of digital invasions as a victim, or you can face the future as a cyber-conscious leader. Now is the time to choose a side.

PART ONE

ASSESSING THE FIELD

1

INFILTRATION IS A GIVEN

VILGINX3 IS a dangerous hacking tool, and anyone can download it from GitHub, the world's largest (and legal) website for open-source code. It is a turnkey solution designed to bypass multifactor authentication defenses and capture a user's session token, the identifier that marks a user's activities as authenticated and trusted. Anyone (assume a cybercriminal) with the credentials and session token can conduct remote activity and appear as a trusted user with access to those systems.

Evilginx3 provides custom phishing lures (phishlets) tuned to various industries, a phishing server to send the phishing lures, a phishing server to capture input credentials, and a phishing server to send those credentials along with the multifactor authentication code to the associated, legitimate authentication service (Google or Microsoft). Evilginx3 captures the session token. From the user's perspective, it's business as usual. They logged in and authenticated, and the related service or application behaved as expected.

In lay terms, one of the security controls we depend on is easily neutralized. Of course, it assumes the user clicks on the phishing lure. The next improvement will enable a man-in-the-middle attack that launches a webpage redirect during normal web browsing. It's another escalation in the arms race between criminals and their potential victims.

Surely, this must be illegal, you might think to yourself. Why doesn't the police or the FBI or even INTERPOL force GitHub to take Evilginx3 off of its server?

The simple answer is that it doesn't matter if GitHub allows open sharing of these kinds of tools. Ostensibly, hacking tools like this are posted on GitHub and elsewhere because developers need to see how phishing works. And to test their defenses. Plenty of "friendly" tools end up in the hands of criminals. Cobalt Strike is another white hat penetration testing tool that became cybercriminals' favorite. As in kinetic war, the weapons we build often end up in our enemy's hands. Using your enemy's strength against them is a page straight out of Sun Tzu's *The Art of War*, proving that strategy outlives technology. And even if law enforcement blocked or somehow controlled access to tools like Evilginx3, similar tools are readily available in dark markets that are much harder to monitor and censor.

The unfortunate reality is that we, the proverbial good guys, have to operate within the confines of the law. Criminals, by their nature, do not. They have the advantage of unfettered tactics, techniques, and procedures.

David Shipley, the CEO and co-founder of Beauceron Security, explains exactly why this takes place.

"It's the curse of Steve Jobs," Shipley explains. "The deliverance of magically consistent user experiences in the Apple platform has made it seem as if it's possible to build a perfect system. We talk about progress. We talk about convenience. We talk about ease of use. We only ever see the good things we want to see. We are cursed with blind hope in technology."

If leaders can't conceptualize the reality of infiltration risk because they assume the internet can be tamed for only the best interests of society, that's a problem.

"Risk can never be completely eliminated as long as you are in a digital world. But the reality is that a lack of understanding of IT instills a false sense of competence in organizational leaders," Shipley says.

If cybersecurity risk can be measured on a scale of 1 to 1,000, where 1 is the lowest level of risk possible and 1,000 is the highest, Shipley explains, organizations will, quite simply, never achieve a score lower than 500. That's because, as he says, having any kind of online presence carries a significant inherent risk that no amount of software can prevent. Unless you decide to return to using paper files, that risk is never going to abate.

We've opened Pandora's box, and there is no going back.

THE FINANCIAL WORLD is more ones and zeroes in the ether than it is cash and precious metals in a vault. Stock exchanges rely on lightspeed connections to extract every ounce of profit from trades and an ever-changing market. Rapid (digital) data sharing between treating physicians, clinicians, and laboratories improves health care and patient outcomes. Students learn from enriched digital video and interactive tutorials. The textbook is rapidly becoming the pay phone of education.

The same thing goes for any business or organization connected to the internet. Like any complex system, the internet is owned by no one group or company. The opportunity for vulnerabilities and flaws is near infinite. Our connection to the internet provides criminals with a similarly infinite number of

The Misfortune 500 are the hacker equivalent of the Fortune 500.

doors and windows in every existing website, email system, and payment protocol. You can put barriers in place, but at some point, the organization becomes impenetrable at the price of halting all operations. It's just not practical in our digital era.

Our leadership blindness is killing our collective ability to deal with infiltration, but the rise of the Misfortune 500, as I call them, compounds the risk.

The Misfortune 500 are the hacker equivalent of the Fortune 500, the best of the best criminal organizations in their field. For every organizational executive with a mission in the business, nonprofit, or government agency, there is an equally well-paid, strategic leader in the hacker world. They lead billion-dollar corporations with C-suites, human resource teams, compensation models, recruiting strategies, and all the bells and whistles you are likely to see in your own organization. They have budgets, targets, and annual reports. They make plans to improve their income streams year over year. They have investors or board-like governors holding positions in their nation's government, military, or intelligence agencies.

They've existed for a while, but it's only in the last five years that these companies have reached the kind of critical mass that allows them to demand ransoms in the multiple millions from unwary victims. That's why, in 2023, 59 percent of organizations reported that they were hit by an attack, according to the Sophos *State of Ransomware* survey.[1] A Washington, DC, cybersecurity firm reports that 76 percent of companies have faced a ransomware attack.[2] On top of that, according to the same survey, the average ransom extorted increased 500 percent in 2023, and those organizations that did pay a ransom paid a median of $2 million. That's up considerably from the previous year, when ransom payments were on average $400,000. The 2024 report also found that 63 percent of ransom demands were for $1 million or more, with 30 percent of demands for over $5 million.

And yet, only 32 percent of these attacks were related to IT system failures. That means that 68 percent of successful ransomware attacks had nothing to do with organizations' primary technology infrastructure (more later on how criminals "live off the land" and exploit open vulnerabilities).

The Misfortune 500 are so successful not because it's incredibly easy to break through IT systems but because their leaders are determined to get what they want. That determination isn't just about money. As you'll discover throughout this book, leaders in the Misfortune 500 have a much bigger stake than cash alone. The Misfortune 500 also fund global conflicts and in some cases, like North Korea, their own government. Organizations that pay ransoms may be inadvertently contributing to the war in Ukraine, to tactical offenses in the South China Sea, and to election fraud in Brazil. That's why, in 2021, the US Treasury explicitly warned that if US organizations paid a ransom to a quasi-governmental actor on their sanctions list, they would be committing a crime by funding terrorism.[3]

Ransomware is no longer a series of random attacks made by random hackers. It is organized and large scale, and it contributes to civil unrest, death, and destruction. By all accounts, ransomware constitutes a war against globalized society. With every line of data we input, someone is watching and waiting to infiltrate our systems. The enemy isn't just looking to steal our money; they're interested in circumventing our businesses, eroding our criminal justice systems and economies, and building distrust in our governments. It's a new Cold War, and there are no borders and no civilians. Everyone in this war is considered a combatant.

We must devise new and better ways of managing ransom demands, and technology alone cannot accomplish that.

THE PROBLEM for leaders is that what we don't know is killing us and our organizations.

Here's why.

We live in a world of distraction, and much has already been said about the chaotic reality in which we have to manage. The military calls this VUCA, an environment characterized by volatility, uncertainty, complexity, and ambiguity. The accelerated development of technologies is compounded by political and social changes, each growing at a dizzying pace.

Organizations must adapt to survive in a VUCA environment to compete in the boundless economy of time and space in worldwide markets that are constantly linked to information typified by complexity and interconnectedness. The evolution of technology blurs the boundaries between countries, organizations, and people; the ability to move among jobs, organizations, and countries is more and more a requirement. New technological and political factors are constantly affecting the working world and changing the rules. We're constantly dealing with information overload with the dissolving of traditional organizational boundaries and business communities. Health problems are increasing, along with extreme weather. Pollution also threatens healthy life, especially for those living in dense urban centers—and more than half the world's population will be living in these kinds of cities before the end of this decade. Stability is also threatened as the gap between rich and poor households grows, polarizing communities on issues of work, education, and urban development. Add to this the different values and expectations of new generations entering the workplace, as well as increased globalization precipitating the need to lead across cultures, and evidence of a VUCA world isn't hard to find.

Business leaders already know that the world is increasingly VUCA, but research shows that most admit they have been recently surprised by at least one VUCA-related event.[4] These leaders cite the fact that predictions for an uncertain future are fraught with problems, so although their organizations need some degree of planning to guide strategic decisions, this is almost impossible.

Tim Evans, former Marine and attorney for the Department of Defense, spent six years at the Maryland branch of the National Security Agency and represented NSA at the White House on the National Security Council. I asked him why he thought that leaders think this way—why they assume the risks don't apply to them.

"I think risk is just not something that they care about. They're moving forward with whatever their business plan entails. If we think about our own life journeys, how each of us manage our day-to-day lives, very few of us plan for battle."

Evans is correct. Whether we run organizations or marathons or rehearsals, we're thinking about our next steps to best practices. We're not thinking about what could happen if someone randomly attacks us in the elevator, on the road, or across the stage.

But we're missing an important point. The way we have traditionally conceptualized cyberattacks is as akin to the risk of getting hit by lightning. In fact, it's not. In the United States, the odds of being struck by lightning in any given year are less than one in a million.[5] In 2024, there were 33.2 million businesses in the United States.[6] In the same year, there were 1,636 cyberattacks per week.[7] The latter number is increasing, but let's do the 2024 math. That means the weekly odds of getting attacked in 2024 was just above 1 in 20,000. That's one hell of a probability difference.

Organizations that expect to operate in VUCA environments will need to develop new skills. Complex environments will reward flexible and responsive collective leadership. These manifest as adaptive competencies such as learning agility, self-awareness, comfort with ambiguity, and strategic thinking. Especially when it comes to cybersecurity, the time is fast approaching for organizations to redress the imbalance that has been created by focusing exclusively on the individual leadership model. We need everyone on board.

So let's get on top of the situation.

2

EVOLVING
BATTLE TACTICS

IR INDUSTRY GIANT Boeing is perhaps as big as a company can get. Maybe that's why the LockBit ransomware gang believed, on October 27, 2023, that a $200 million ransom was not an unreasonable ask.

The LockBit ransomware group captured only 43 gigabytes of Boeing company data. LockBit achieved this via a small vulnerability in the company's secure remote access system, affecting all organizations using Citrix-managed cloud services for this purpose, not just Boeing. LockBit set a November 2 deadline for payment. When that deadline passed without Boeing caving to their demands, LockBit warned the company that it would release 4 gigabytes as a sample of what had been stolen. They did so, and then a week later, they released the rest. The aerospace company refused to pay any part of the ransom, the highest-ever demand from a ransomware organization.

LockBit was likely testing the waters with no real expectation of receiving the full ransom. With 2,500 proven victims, including nearly 1,800 in the United States, LockBit is a full-scale enterprise-level organization that has targeted law enforcement agencies, security firms, municipalities, schools, financial organizations, and even multinational fast-food chains.

Ransomware is crowdsourced warfare. It's different from outmoded tactics that rely on the genius of individual hackers. As we've seen with Evilginx3, open-source code can be downloaded and dropped into the field almost instantly, targeting millions of companies, organizations, and users simultaneously. But code like Evilginx3 is small-scale in comparison to what the Misfortune 500 is up to.

The reality is that LockBit primarily attacks US and other Western corporations because of the group's links to Russian governmental entities. They are not alone in doing so—LockBit is only one such company. FIN7, DarkSide, TA505, and Royal/BlackSuit, the latter of which was born out of the remains of the notorious Conti group of cybercriminals, are among the leading ransomware groups in the world. And yet, because our media calls them "gangs" in news reports, we completely underestimate the power and the perils of these organizations.

They aren't gangs. They're operatives. They're organizations. They have more in common with a global intelligence agency than they do with a group of thugs fighting a turf war to retain their street credibility.

Robert Johnston is an expert at conducting counterespionage engagements against nation-state, criminal, and hacktivist organizations, and a former US Marine Corps team leader of the 81 National Cyber Protection Team, Cyber National Mission Force, and director of the Red Team.

"While most criminals use the funds for profit rather than feeding terrorists, the situation is more nuanced than that," Johnston says. "Russian intelligence agencies are not interested in the money that's collected from that ransomware group. Their purpose in collaborating with ransomware organizations is to inflict damage on the target. It's a proxy war method."

Because our media
calls them "gangs," we
completely underestimate
the power and the perils
of these organizations.

Kristen Farnum, who was a conflict management advisor and ceasefire monitor in Ukraine for the Organization for Security and Co-operation in Europe and formerly worked with the US Department of Defense and State Department for deployments in Afghanistan and Iraq, agrees.

"Americans can't understand Russian ideology. Russia is seen as divine, and restoring the territory to its czarist glory is paramount. Russia benefits from arm's-length activities with ransomware organizations simply because it weakens the West," she explains. "Add to that the fact that it's a thugocracy, and the rules of war that we're used to simply don't apply." Worse yet, she warns, "we underestimate the power of neural shaping when it comes to nationalist propaganda."

The same can be said of Chinese hacking actors, with perhaps an even more substantial link between cybercriminals and the state. In January 2024, the FBI executed a protocol to disinfect Microsoft Exchange servers compromised by a China-state group tracked as Hafnium. This followed years of Chinese government attacks against US routers, cameras, and other network-connected devices, aiming to target critical infrastructure and establish persistent access into US networks.[1]

These alliances between rival governments and cybercriminals may be tacit or explicit, but they amount to the same thing: a deliberative aim to weaken a Western, and specifically an American, way of life. That's why solving the problem isn't easy. Sure, it's about the illegal exchange of money, but it's more than that. This kind of cybercrime is about values and principles: theirs are very different than ours. Add to this the fact that, because of the chasm between values, Russia is never going to shut down its cybercrime organizations, and it won't comply with international warrants and charges. China is going to continue to breach US security, according to the FBI. Not only that, but China and Russia are also taking stances against each other in a bid for global hegemony. North Korea and Iran are background players picking up the scraps. And other countries are likely to follow suit as ransomware-as-a-service (RaaS) becomes even more ubiquitous, making solving the problem all the more complex.

FOR LEADERS, knowing this status quo, there are choices to be made.

To date, most CEOs have chosen just to pay ransoms, because they see this as a business problem to solve. CEO of Eclipse Automation Steve Mai did just that back in 2019.

"You can negotiate as a victim or negotiate as a business-person," he explains, detailing the ransomware attack that slowed his operations to a halt.

"I was in our German facility when I got the phone call on Halloween," Mai says. "The attack was pretty severe. I mean, we had backup servers and backup tapes, but it wasn't enough. Our insurance company made us pivot to another cybersecurity company to negotiate, but we were losing in the region of $650,000 per day. Speed to recovery was my primary goal."

Mai was lucky. He had a cash-positive company with no debt or shareholders. He could make decisions on the fly, and so paying out a $4 million ransom was the right thing to do to keep his business afloat. At the time, it was the only thing to do.

But that didn't mean that the situation was easy.

Michelle Sangster was a senior executive at Eclipse when the ransomware attack took place. "Being in that situation wasn't shocking, but it was harrowing," she says. "We needed to get people to reduce their stress and gain a sense of control, the equivalent of chopping wood and carrying water."

The team was huddled in a war room to try all of the angles, working around the clock. Because the police hadn't been notified, an employee tried reporting the fact that his personal data was stolen, but that didn't work. The Bitcoin exchange was botched, and the company thought briefly that they had lost millions. In some ways, as Mai and Sangster explain, Eclipse was held hostage twice: once by the criminals and a second time by the insurance process. The insurance company was searching for proof of Eclipse's negligence so that they wouldn't have to pay out.

Despite the frantic events of the attack, Eclipse's customers were, luckily, very understanding. Mai discovered that the more transparent he was with his stakeholders, the more likely he was to get the support he needed. Because the company had a culture of solving problems for a living, that was a major advantage. They communicated updates daily and ensured that everyone was on the same side.

"Cybercrime is a crime that you have to self-manage. You're on your own," Mai says, knowing that no one from the criminal justice system stepped in to help him when he reported the incident to police. "And you can't move on until you get back up and running."

Mai is right in one way and wrong in another. Unlike his level of autonomy, most leaders are surrounded by impatient board members, eager law enforcement agencies, and even government representatives. But we'll get to these points later in the book.

Later, Mai found out that the $4 million went directly to Conti.

During the 2022 Russian invasion of Ukraine, Conti announced its support of Russia and threatened to deploy retaliatory measures if cyberattacks were launched against the country, as Farnum explains. Prior to the war, Conti had built up major resources and operations within Ukraine. That's why Europol, the shared European law enforcement group from The Hague, worked with the National Police of Ukraine and seven national justice organizations in a coordinated raid on thirty properties in Kyiv, Cherkasy, Rivne, Vinnytsia, and other cities to bring Conti down. This resulted in the arrest of operatives as well as five key figures, the equivalent of their C-suite, behind Conti's ransomware operations.[2]

Even though Conti was, at least temporarily, shut down, Mai's money likely funded months of anti-Ukraine misinformation within Russia, as well as the proliferation of cyberattacks within Ukraine. Via Conti, the GRU, Russia's military intelligence agency, conducted sophisticated cyberattacks on Ukraine's critical infrastructure both before and after the full-scale invasion of 2022, but even more recently, it has been shown that the Kremlin believes it is in a shadow war with NATO.[3]

We all should collectively be grateful for Boeing's choice not to pay their ransom demand. Even though Boeing's decision was informed by their business strategy alone, in light of the Conti operations, it's clear there is more at stake than money. All of this is why it makes sense that Western governments are paying more attention to those organizations that choose to pay ransoms to operations housed in countries on their sanctions list.

And yet, I don't blame Mai for his choice. The necessity to protect his business was front and center. How the ransom funds might be used was more nebulous and certainly not top of mind. We shouldn't judge. It's a no-win situation.

While, at the time that Mai paid his ransom, tracing the money trail may not have been a simple thing, it is now. Now we know. Governments and organizations such as Europol are clear that paying ransomware is not about paying some hacker living in his parents' basement. Right now, organizations that pay out are likely, in fact, funding terrorism and even war. That means that organizations that pay out are likely committing crimes themselves.

Leaders need to take heed. The US Department of the Treasury has warned as much in a series of advisories.[4]

3

BUILDING RISK AWARENESS

"**THIS IS MY** *Jurassic Park* analogy," David Shipley explained to me. He was referring to the film based on the Michael Crichton book in which industrialist John Hammond builds a park for cloned dinosaurs on the remote fictional island of Isla Nublar, far away from human contact. Everything is wonderful until it isn't, and suddenly the many species of dinosaurs are escaping into the wild, putting the whole world at risk.

"The John Hammond fallacy proves one thing. Small changes can lead to unintended repeated failures that we do not see coming. It's a fallacy that we can build ever more complex systems and maintain control over those systems. In *Jurassic Park*, to think that there's no way possible that a T. rex is ever going to eat me is folly. The same is true for technological security."

As a researcher and consultant with decades of experience, of course Shipley is correct. Both *Jurassic Park* and technology equally illustrate chaos theory and the hubris that comes from believing technology of any sort is perfect. As we build more and more software, we unintentionally add more layers of abstraction and complexity.

At the same time, Shipley argues, leaders' false sense of security competence is increasing as we begin to rely on technology on a broad cultural level.

"Security culture is the sum of the norms and values believed, communicated, and expressed in everyday actions and choices," he explains. "But we're running headlong into risk because we may not have fully understood what that risk was."

What is that risk?

"If John Hammond had expressed empathy and compassion and offered an olive branch to the people who were warning him about what could go wrong, we'd be looking at a different outcome in *Jurassic Park*. In the same way, there are human solutions to cyber problems, and how we treat other human beings has a direct relationship with cyber risk."

WE OFTEN try to understand risk as a mathematical equation balancing ideas like financial equity, reward, and supply and demand. What we don't talk about nearly often enough is the reality of the human equation when it comes to cybersecurity.

As we've already discussed, with the rise of cybercrime and its link to global changes in sociopolitical movements, there are new fundamental risks for organizations connected to their geographic location, their social context, and even their symbolic value to attackers. These are all human problems, not technological ones. There is a clear and present danger in which cybercrime is connected to geopolitical decisions based on vast global divides in ideology.

But there is also a significant inherent risk to organizations who forget their own internal human equation.

Tracy Wareing Evans served as a senior advisor to US Department of Homeland Security secretary Janet Napolitano, with responsibilities for liaising with the Federal Emergency Management Agency; as director of the Arizona Department of Economic Security; and as section chief counsel for Child Protective Services in Arizona. If anyone knows how to mitigate human risk, it's Evans.

"We have to normalize risk assessment in everything that we do," Evans explains. "And to understand your risks, you have to be vulnerable. Leaders have to be able to say, 'I don't know the answer.' The most significant risk we can incur is when a leader assumes that an emergency won't happen to them."

But the biggest barrier to addressing risks, according to Evans, is that human factor.

And let's be clear: while, technically, everyone in an organization presents a possible security risk, the top of the organization is where the problem often lies. Just like in the John Hammond fallacy, leaders do not admit their own vulnerabilities. Yes, it's possible that a newly hired intern may open a phishing email that leads to a cascade of criminal activity. However, what may be even more important to the cybersecurity equation is a CEO who doesn't take the time to listen to their IT team when they recommend a cybersecurity training program for all new hires that would prevent phishing success in the first place. That's why leaders not only have to take responsibility fast, but they also have to take responsibility *first*.

Vince Molinaro is the *New York Times*–bestselling author of five books on leadership, and his research aligns directly with Evans's experience.

"I think there's something in the human psyche about risk that suggests that when we think about tangible risk like the loss of life during natural disasters, we plan ahead and rally to

What we don't talk about often enough is the human equation when it comes to cybersecurity.

the occasion. But when it comes to cyberevents, it's intangible, so we don't take the risk seriously."

Molinaro is correct. Just because leaders think technology is outside their wheelhouse, they can't assume everything is wonderful until it isn't. In fact, admitting that they do not understand the risk is the very reason that leaders have to connect with their teams more often and take the time to listen.

"Building relationships before a crisis takes place is critical," Evans tells me. "Team members need to be able to tell leaders difficult things. If they can't do that when there is no emergency, how are they going to succeed when time is of the essence? Acting like a leader, you have to help your entire team communicate, connect, and create openness to critical thinking before you face an external threat."

IF THE HUMAN EQUATION is critical to risk awareness, then as cybersecurity threat levels evolve for organizations, there is a need for a shift in leadership thinking. A shift from VUCA to VUCA Prime, if you will.

Author Bob Johansen of the Institute for the Future proposed this new way of thinking.[1] VUCA Prime turns VUCA upside down. In this model, everything flips to shift VUCA awareness to VUCA leadership.

Vision replaces volatility. In constant change, organizations must have a clear and adaptable vision that guides their actions. Creating a clear vision serves as a compass, helping them stay on course even when the business environment is turbulent.

Understanding replaces uncertainty. Rather than being paralyzed by uncertainty, leaders should seek a deeper understanding of what is affecting their organization and how they might better relate to what is happening on a broad scale.

Clarity replaces complexity. In a complex world, clarity becomes a prized asset. Leaders must strive to eliminate ambiguity, provide clear and decisive directions, and avoid situations with multiple interpretations. Leaders need to simplify the complexities, communicate effectively, and ensure that everyone in the organization understands the overarching goals and strategies.

Agility replaces ambiguity. Instead of being confounded by ambiguity, organizations should embrace agility. This means shifting toward best practices in innovation and reflecting on who has the right information at the right time.

Thinking about VUCA in these terms ensures that we don't become overloaded with fear during a time of crisis. In fact, it's about predicting and preventing crises rather than assuming that the inevitable will never happen to our own organizations.

Risk, even in human terms, is something that leaders can measure and mitigate, but that process starts with becoming aware of their own limitations. It starts with reaching out for help, not hiding behind insurance policies.

In the next section of this book, you're going to learn about what your organization needs to build a base of operations. Together, we'll pinpoint the risk metrics that really matter.

PART TWO

BUILDING A BASE OF OPERATIONS

4

RESPECTING THE TECHNOLOGY BASELINE

N THE PROVINCE of British Columbia, one of the largest economies in Canada, seventy-six cybersecurity experts are employed year-round simply to protect government systems from cyberattacks at a cost of more than $25 million (US$18 million) a year in addition to their baseline IT operations team. That's because a number of attempts are made on these systems daily, Premier David Eby has stated, just like on many other governments around the world.[1]

These systems were breached on April 11, 2024, and again twice the following month.

Along with the province's internal team, the Canadian Centre for Cyber Security and Microsoft's Detection and Response Team worked quickly to address what was assumed to be an attack orchestrated by a group of independent hackers working for an unnamed foreign government. Forty terabytes of data were infiltrated, more than the amount held in the US Library of Congress. This attack came hard on the heels of other well-publicized infiltrations in the province. The BC Libraries Cooperative reported that on April 19 it was contacted by a hacker attempting to extort payment using private information taken from its servers, and the leading pharmacy chain London Drugs closed its doors for almost a week after dealing with similar threats during the same time window.

The series of attacks, to the British Columbian public, felt like a deluge. The premier and organizational leaders affected by these infiltrations provided studied and careful messages to media sources. They outlined what had happened, who was involved, and what was being done to protect the public. But the relentless nature of these attacks on the westernmost region of Canada was disturbing and no doubt eroded the trust between exhausted citizens and their government.

It is so disturbing because the province, like most governments in North America and Europe, has made huge investments in technological tools. Similar to the Boeing story in Chapter 2 and those of other organizations its size, British Columbia has the ability to reach its vendors and federal agencies on speed dial. Government agencies and Fortune 500 firms aren't suffering from a lack of knowledge or attention to training. All public servants change their passwords weekly and are trained to identify and report phishing schemes.

And yet, in 2023, the FBI received a record number of complaints from the American public, with 880,418 complaints with potential losses exceeding $12.5 billion, which is nearly a 10 percent increase in complaints and a 22 percent increase in losses compared to 2022. And it's not just the United States suffering. In the United Kingdom, as of January 2023, around 37 percent of large companies had experienced cybercrime within the past year.[2] And 44 percent of United Arab Emirates retailers experienced cyberattacks or data breaches in 2023, a significant 39 percent jump compared to figures from 2022.[3] Globally, cybercrime now happens every nine seconds, and many digital criminals are patient, waiting until they collect the right combination of data before selling it to someone who will use it for nefarious purposes, which means these figures will only increase over time.[4]

The reason these challenges are converging is obvious to authorities.

On May 14, 2024, the Government of Canada's cyberspy agency, the Communications Security Establishment, issued a warning in a joint advisory with the United States, the United Kingdom, Japan, Estonia, and Finland that Russia, China, Iran, and North Korea are increasingly targeting nonprofit and advocacy groups, as well as journalists and human rights activists.[5] Targeted civil society groups also include academic, cultural, and diaspora organizations and individuals working to advance democracy. Governments, libraries, universities, and pharmacies all fall within this spectrum of targets. Instead of ransomware, threat actors are using increasingly personalized and subversive tactics, devoting significant resources to researching their targets.

At the same time, global law enforcement capacity has not yet come to terms with the huge network of attackers spread out in diverse global locations who communicate with each other through hidden means.

For example, in Canada, a 2024 auditor general's report found that federal law enforcement services lacked the capacity needed to deal with growing cyberthreats. "This impaired the federal policing branch's ability to understand the full picture of cybercrime cases reported to its cybercrime unit and to keep track of specific cases assigned to the unit for investigation," the report found. Moreover, the report noted "breakdowns in response, coordination, enforcement, tracking, and analysis between and across the organizations responsible for protecting Canadians from cybercrime." To this end, the auditor general said, "Without prompt action, financial and personal information losses will only grow as the volume of cybercrime and attacks continues to increase."[6]

I'd wager that these law enforcement challenges aren't limited to Canada.

Even if a government such as that of the United States identifies a hacker and brings charges, that individual may be out of reach of their own local courts, which means that most cases tend to be civil rather than criminal, and they take years to play out. On top of this, organized crime syndicates are not just businesses; they are linked to and often incorporated into government activities that cannot be prosecuted.

The extent to which cybercrime intersects with the law is also broad. In the United States, the Department of Justice has for decades defined computer crime as any illegal act for which knowledge of computer technology is essential.[7] The DoJ has been prosecuting computer crime since the late 1970s. Nonetheless, some of the problems in pursuing an effective prosecution involve the fact that cybernetworks are so difficult to infiltrate, and many of them are even automated, making it difficult to trace the crime back to a single location or person.

They also overlap. Cybercrime can involve identity theft, embezzlement, fraud, and outright theft. This can occur via malicious code, a Distributed Denial of Service (DDoS) attack, spam fraud, phishing for information, or even using Google-like searches (called SEO poisoning) to identify popular data sources used by potential victims. It can also involve higher-level financial fraud, such as corporate security breaches, piracy, and large-scale consumer information theft, which can

Never assume that the company at the center of a headline ended up there because of negligence.

put millions of people at risk simultaneously. It can be committed through fraud, deception, or collusion, and it can include activities such as money laundering or organizational fraud, committed on behalf of a client as well as for personal gain. Whether physical crime or virtual (cyber) crime, the motivators and opportunities are the same. Worse, cryptocurrency and the broader financial fabric make it easier to use criminal gains to fund existential threats, including terrorism.

All of this means that, in the cyberworld, there are few rules and fewer convictions, and neither national nor international laws can keep up. For example, according to the FBI's *2023 Internet Crime Report*, nearly 304,000 cyberfraud complaints led to just 1,400 criminal cases (far less than 1 percent) and six convictions—one for every 51,000 victims.[8] International law enforcement cooperation, especially INTERPOL warrants, can take months to deploy, giving the criminals ample getaway time.[9]

It is critical for leaders to really grasp our new reality, namely that even with the best technology in place and the most dedicated super-experts on their teams, organizations will come up against devastating attacks. Never assume that the company at the center of a headline ended up there because of negligence or a laissez-faire approach to cybersecurity.

EVEN SO, and despite international government warnings, all organizations still have to try to hold the line.

The baseline set of technological tools that every organization needs to put into play is, by and large, determined by insurers. If you do not meet these criteria, you may fall short of the threshold for support, and that's not a situation you want to face. That's why getting your baseline protections in good shape is critical.

Kirsten Bay is the CEO of Cysurance, a company that underwrites cyber insurance policies, certifies warrants, and insures security solutions deployed by enterprise end users. She has over twenty-five years of experience in risk intelligence, information management, and policy work. As Bay says, set parameter controls are satisfied by products' checks and balances. Think about the security features offered by Microsoft that protect companies from many attacks or those that are hard-coded into firewall software. Encryption is standard; it's embedded in every layer.

But knowing that encryption exists is not enough. Leaders need to pay attention to the basics if they want to be covered by their insurers.

"Leaders should be thinking about their technological tools in the same way they think about driving a car," Bay explains. "Product controls are your cyber-seatbelt. A seatbelt itself does a really good job protecting you. In a car, you can also invest in additional safety features like airbags and anti-lock brakes and lane drift alerts, but if you don't have your cyber-seatbelt clicked in, you're still going to put your life at risk."

Many companies purchase great software with fundamental protections but don't click them into place, and they don't continue managing them. Or worse, they ignore vendor guidance because leaders don't understand the value of this advice. In many cases, unclear division of duties between customer and vendor leads to proverbial dropped balls. Criminals become the benefactors of such misplays.

For example, every security vendor out there will advise using multifactor authentication (MFA). This multistep account login process requires users to enter more information than just a password. For example, along with the password, users must enter a code sent via an authenticated email or text message, or scan a fingerprint on their phone. MFA introduces an additional level of complexity, such as something you know (a PIN or codeword), something you possess (a key, smartphone, or token device), or something you are (fingerprint, facial recognition, or retinal scans). This complexity makes it harder for criminals to use stolen account credentials. They might have your username and password, but they don't have your smartphone and won't receive the SMS text message sent at login. But adding MFA costs time, even if it's embedded in software and doesn't cost money, and there are many leaders who just don't bother. All too often complexity (security) comes at the cost of convenience. In companies of fewer than one hundred employees, only one in three have adopted MFA.[10]

And that's just stupid.

Imagine complaining about the hardship of having to unlock your car every time you want to go for a drive. It's more about familiarity and baseline expectations than convenience.

"Not bothering to turn on MFA, in one case we investigated, resulted in a high-severity incident," Bay recalls. "I remember just sitting and scratching my head and asking the CEO, 'What were you thinking? Your company does background checks and has security guards. Why didn't you have MFA on your email? All of your data is gone.'"

THE BASICS MATTER.

I'm not going to give you technological advice here, because, as when you're driving a car, your mileage will definitely vary. You will need technological tools specific to your industry, your budget, the size and scope of your organization, and your insurers' needs.

"What's frightening about it is that organizations are so wrapped around their own axle on ransomware that they don't realize that addressing these fundamentals represents a much greater threat to them," Bay says. "Buying into a false sense of invulnerability results in a sidestepping of accountability."

As a leader, you are responsible to your organization, shareholders, and customers. Your stakeholders rely on your ability to maintain your data integrity. Bay underlines the substantive business consequences of not paying attention to and respecting the technology baseline. Once these fundamentals are in place, you can create a workable, strong incident response plan.

To understand what your organization requires, you need to listen to your IT team members and vendors.

Consider the K–12 education districts turned on their heads by the COVID-19 pandemic. In the wake of shelter-from-home directives, the US federal government funded remote learning infrastructure as part of the $190 million Elementary and Secondary School Emergency Relief Fund. That was during the pandemic. Years later, those systems and hardware are reaching their obsolescence. Yet, no funding will be forthcoming to support updates. Lack of patching and out-of-date systems leave doors wide open for criminals.

Miguel Hablutzel is an expert in vulnerability management and helping business leaders understand the risk associated with the potential exploits of these open doors. He started his career in the Peruvian Navy and then moved to the United States, where he pursued his passion for technology.

"Once you understand a risk, you can either remediate, transfer, or accept the risk," he told me in a recent conversation. As Hablutzel explained, monthly comparisons of the same customers exposed lingering vulnerabilities. Rather than assuming leaders leave his risk reports unread, he attributed patching lethargy to a sense of overwhelm and lack of a practical way forward. Moreover, business leaders don't equate vulnerabilities with fiduciary exposures.

"The cost of not taking action is far more costly than patching solutions," he said. "More and more, insurers refuse to pay out claims when they discover exposed and unpatched systems."

To make informed decisions, you have to set aside your assumptions about where you should be spending money on your IT infrastructure, and trust your team. Business culture is fraught with false narratives and bravado. One such claim is the need to be the smartest person in the room. In fact, the smartest (wisest?) leaders surround themselves with people who know more than they do. Surround yourself with experts. And listen to them.

As retired United Airlines captain Al Haynes recounted following the survival of a catastrophic engine failure and subsequent crash-landing of United Airlines Flight 232, crew resource management (CRM) was pivotal. When facing a situation novel to your organization, like a cyberattack, no one is an expert, and everyone's opinion matters. CRM methodologies are used in high-risk industries, including aviation, medicine, and mining, to foster a less authoritarian culture and drive collaboration. Haynes praised CRM as the difference between life and death. Take his word for it.

To ensure that your bases are covered, you need to follow the *experts'* rules, not your own.

5

ACKNOWLEDGING THE DISCONNECT

"THE STATE, AND by that I mean any government, collects more data than they should," Deborah Snyder says. "They don't routinely purge big data. They often don't know where their data is, or where it travels, or who they share it with, because there are thousands of data-sharing agreements between agencies."

Snyder is a senior fellow at the Center for Digital Government, which she became after retiring from her position as New York State's chief information security officer (CISO) and following over thirty-five years of public service, directing the NYS Cyber Command Center, hotline, procedures for reporting and response to cyberthreats, and digital forensics.

If we follow the data, we can see exactly what Snyder is talking about.

"Think about federal tax," Snyder points out. "An individual's tax status is shared by the IRS with each US state. The state, of course, shares data in the other direction. Add to this all of the data touchpoints with counties and agencies, such as each state Board of Elections. Then, there are data links between the federal systems, state systems, and county systems that connect with contracts and third parties. Finally, the tax data needs to connect to citizens who pay taxes and need copies of their federal and state tax returns, and companies who file electronic paperwork about each employee. At the same time, by extension, employment and social service management; public health; 911 systems; federal, state, and local crime and judicial systems; dispatch; health and human services; resources; and emergency management all connect at some point to the same data stream."

In my experience in the field, I can say that the same is true for the business sector, perhaps even more so. Unlike governments, businesses don't have constraints on how or why they collect and use data.

As Snyder explains, these data streams create dependencies. Upstream, you have data dependencies for yourself; downstream, you have organizations dependent on your data. Where the rubber hits the road is the risk created by these dependencies. The more you have, the more likely that someone, somewhere, will find the right place to breach your defenses.

WE ARE ADDICTED to data. We believe data can and will solve business problems, ease public service issues, and make us more money. We collect and use client and customer data; human resource data; market, health, education, and systems data; and more. With the rise of AI, we believe the possibilities for advancing our strategies are endless.

As Snyder brilliantly illustrates, our reliance on data makes us vulnerable. The more data we collect and use, the more vulnerable we are.

Big data offers a way of fulfilling consumer needs in an interconnected world. By tracking purchases of products and services globally and gathering information on aggregate and personal consumer spending patterns, companies can tailor all marketing factors to potential and current customers, from price to product attributes to advertising. Information, including internal and external data and consumer, supplier, and competitor data, can be merged to increase revenue. The use of end-to-end digital processes can also decrease costs.

As I've written before, the consumer is the product in our digital world.[1]

Take the example of loyalty programs. You've definitely got a card for your grocery store, airline, bookstore, or pharmacy that throws a minimal discount or cash back to you if you spend a thousand dollars in their store. You may have even spearheaded this kind of program if you're a business leader. But what does that company get in return? Both personalized and aggregate marketing data entice customers to spend more and more in stores and keep them from going to competitors.

But it could also be argued that loyalty programs aren't sustainable. From an economic point of view, they decrease competition and they rely on customers to do the hard work for them, reacting to that tiny carrot they're dangling. From a cybersecurity point of view, they expose companies to increased risk. Remember the pharmacy in British Columbia that had to shut down for a week, mentioned in the previous chapter? They were targeted precisely because they collected that consumer data. That's what made their company attractive to hackers.

It's absolutely true that big data and integrated data can power businesses to increase profits. It's also absolutely true that big data presents big holes in our security systems, leading to massive financial losses.

Chaos theory looks at unpredictable results that can come from the interaction of complex factors, with a ripple that starts somewhere, increases in intensity, and changes direction as

Regulations reflect threats of the past. By the time they are implemented, criminals have moved on to another paradigm of attack.

it moves throughout space and time. Each data point in our systems, this theory suggests, is bombarded by countless tiny forces within its immediate vicinity. In nature, when we repeat patterns endlessly, they do not stay the same. When chaos theory is applied to cybersecurity, we begin to understand that no matter how much we try to control things, the infinite changes brought on by new technologies are very much controlled by increasingly unpredicted outcomes, infinitely complex and twisting in different directions than we expected. Technology helps us obtain more information more quickly, driving better, faster, easier, and cheaper ways to mine it.

But each side—namely those who live within the law and those who choose to break it—acts to outpace the other and gain an invisible advantage. Each side, whether through legal or illegal means, has evolved its approach to data through engineered solutions that facilitate access to money. As a result, organizations must be able to navigate the chaos and decide what is most important to them.

WHAT DATA are you collecting, and why? I'm not going to argue that organizations return to the 1980s in order to stay safe. But there is a need to be strategic about data collection and storage and your justification for it. The European Union's General Data Protection Regulation begins with this premise.

This need for a data strategy isn't just about staying safe from ransoms and thefts, either. Western legal frameworks are moving toward a system that places the onus on the criminal justice system to deter crime through punishment. As a result, policies are going to be created to dry up the demand for data in the first place rather than prosecuting crimes, according to Jeff Kosseff, associate professor of cybersecurity law at the United States Naval Academy.[2] This places an extra legal burden on external actors, such as corporations and organizations like hospitals, to control the way in which they create, use, and sell data that is linked to customer accounts. Organizations sanctioned under this new framework will have to contend with legal frameworks that hold them responsible. Connected to this issue is the tendency for government agencies, regulators, law enforcement arms, and standards councils to build legal and regulatory mechanisms aimed at large enterprises where resources are far more abundant, in-house expertise is more likely, and budgets flow from large reserves, leaving many citizens and smaller organizations unprotected.

Remember, regulations and guidelines reflect threats of the past. By the time they are implemented, criminals have moved on to another stomping ground or paradigm of attack. Moreover, regulations, or compliance, does not equal security. Consider the RMS *Titanic*. She was compliant with the maritime laws of the time, yet we know what happened on the maiden voyage of the ship considered virtually unsinkable.

So what can you do to approach data strategically? Snyder recommends five key strategies to achieve your goals:

1 Maintain a data asset inventory so you know what information you need to protect and what state it is in.

2 Set priorities for data sets, and create timelines for data removal.

3 Track data ownership, business uses, and associated security and privacy requirements for each data set.

4 Build a strategic road map to decide what data you do and do not need over the course of time.

5 Continuously assess data to identify and delete unneeded data packets, reducing opportunities for attackers to target weaknesses.

6

CLOSING RANKS

"**WHAT WE OFTEN FORGET,**" Bob Darling says, "is that leaders have to be comfortable in their own skin, not in their titles. Mature leadership means listening to your experts. Tell them what you need, but don't tell them how to do their jobs."

Darling should know. A US Marine since 1978, he is a former Super Cobra attack helicopter pilot, and he flew Marine One (the president's helicopter) for three administrations. He was stationed as the White House airlift operations leader during 9/11. Darling was a part of the White House evacuation—for only the second time in history, 187 years after it was burned to the ground by British soldiers during the War of 1812. As the liaison between Vice President Dick Cheney in the president's bunker and the Pentagon as events unfolded in September 2001, all while President George W. Bush was on Air Force One and unreachable on communications, Darling exercised his leadership skills under the most harrowing conditions.

Given what he's seen go down over the kind of career he's had, Darling's not wrong about what it takes to lead in a crisis and what contributes to failure.

Donald Rumsfeld, secretary of defense, happened to be at the Pentagon when the E Ring was struck by American Airlines Flight 77 at approximately 9:37 a.m., its path of destruction ending in the alley between the C and B Rings. Having a very human reaction, given what had happened, Rumsfeld was out in the parking lot assisting with evacuating the wounded. And yet, Rumsfeld was one of the two people who had National Command Authority over the military, the other being President Bush. With Bush on Air Force One, Rumsfeld was supposed to be giving the orders, but he wasn't at the national military command center, the War Room.

Somebody had to tell American pilots how to defend the country.

Vice President Cheney started making those calls in Bush's and Rumsfeld's absence. He knew the protocols in place because he used to be the secretary of defense. At the same time, there was a gap in the chain of command. The military was not supposed to take orders from the vice president unless the president was dead and the Twenty-Fifth Amendment to the US Constitution had been officially enacted.

"We had two F-16s on alert in Langley, Virginia, right nearby, but Vice President Cheney said, 'I want the two F-15s in Massachusetts,'" Darling explains. "We literally left the two F-16s sitting on the runway waiting for orders at half the distance, of course, but because Vice President Cheney called for the other fighters hundreds of miles away, we had to deploy them. We didn't know the reason, and neither did the operator making the call."

It didn't make sense then, and it still doesn't make sense to Darling now. It's possible that Cheney simply didn't know about the planes sitting close at hand, or relied on previous knowledge from previous posts with the administration. But, to Darling watching what was going down, it was a leadership lesson.

"When you're a part of the C-suite, you're not a tactical person anymore. You shouldn't be making those tactical decisions and demands," he says. "Tell me you want fighters, and let the people who are best placed to do so determine how to use the resources available."

Darling suggests that the typical power triangle, which has a single CEO and small C-suite at the top and all employees at the bottom, should be flipped upside down. This is especially true in a time of crisis, and he gives an example of someone who did things right.

"Dr. Condoleezza Rice, our national security advisor, was in the bunker during 9/11," Darling goes on to say. "She let military members do what we do best. She stood behind us and asked us what we needed to get things done. It was an exercise in trust and in the delegation of authority. She would have gotten me a bottle of water if I had asked for it. She was so humble, and yet so powerful."

Those on the front lines, even people on a help desk, are the people with their eyes on a crisis event, Darling explains.

"You've got to believe in them and give them the authority to take immediate steps. And, you know, that's tough for people to do. But crisis leadership is about compartmentalization," Darling reminds us. "You do the job that needs to be done and you block out everything else. You're not taking notes, you're not answering the phone, you're doing exactly what needs to be done. Leadership starts with a very narrow window of focus, and then, as you get control of the situation, you can widen that aperture."

WHEN IT COMES TO cybersecurity, you have to shift the way you think about leadership fundamentally. Your role as a leader is crucial to your organization's survival. But that leadership role may have to look very different from what you imagine.

John Caruthers worked for the FBI for twenty-seven years, retiring in 2019 after a career spent investigating cybercriminals. He's now a consultant advising large organizations on how to protect their cyber gates from invasion. He offers the same warnings about leadership as Darling. Organizational leaders want to shut down costs, so they see IT people as problems to solve, not experts to respect.

"I have spent a lot of time trying to convince leadership and finance that we need to invest in security. They don't, because they can't monetize it. It's been more of a nice-to-have than a requirement. Now, because of regulations, privacy law, and insurance policies, we have a lot of compelling reasons to shift that discussion," Caruthers explains. "But the C-suite, the board, executive leadership, they still don't know how to talk about what they see as 'nerd' stuff."

That perceived social distinction between the cool guys at the top of the food chain and the so-called nerds is a common cultural dynamic in organizations, and it has to go.

James Lin, CISO for the Regional Municipality of Halton in Ontario, Canada, agrees.

"You have to talk to the line staff to get the situation on the ground instead of waiting for a consultant to give you the rose-colored view of things," Lin says.

This means that there is a strategic need for risk management, and that starts with talking to people who are actually dealing with round-the-clock cyber risks. As both Caruthers and Lin underline, leaders can't avoid these conversations. In fact, leaders should embrace these opportunities. As the saying often attributed to the UK prime minister Winston Churchill goes, "Never let a good crisis go to waste."

Think about this for a moment.

Organizational leaders keep telling their teams that they need to innovate, to disrupt, to be brave. But their employees lack the support and the tools to do just that. Patrick Lencioni's five dysfunctions of a team—lack of trust, fear of conflict, lack of commitment, avoidance of accountability, and inattention

Leaders have to
be comfortable in
their own skin,
not in their titles.

to results—are all affected by a lack of curiosity and of support on the part of leaders.[1] The reality within organizations is that most social norms are so entrenched that people don't feel as if they can come forward with questions about what is possible, let alone answers.

In a cybercrisis, who makes the decisions: The senior person? The technical expert? The self-appointed hero? The person with the right answer or critical piece of information will often remain quiet among a throng of Type-A extroverts. In crisis leadership, removing the emotion around who is allowed to make decisions is critical. Yet our human biases, office politics, and perceived personal fears often influence or delay sound decision-making.

Teams perform a special role: they allow operations with multiple stakeholders the opportunity to create plans that aim to meet everyone's needs, rather than relying on a leader alone to provide structure, which is why they are so important during times of crisis. We know that team members need to feel supported to really get curious, because they need to feel it is okay and right and normal to share thoughts and ideas that deviate from what leaders expect them to say. Even more so, we leaders need to tell ourselves that following the lead of our employees is the right thing to do.

Cybercrime will not be solved with magic tech solutions; it will be solved by fundamentally great leadership, as Tim Evans explains.

"Working in the most offensive organization within the NSA, I went to a conference for my unit in Estonia in 2009," Evans told me. "And while I'm at this conference, I met Johannes Kert, who was the commander of the Estonian Defence Forces. He was the head of our state partnership there."

In his youth, Kert had been forced to serve as lieutenant in the Soviet Army, starting with two obligatory years of service before being assigned to remote Soviet military units. Many in his unit, Evans shared with me, remembered Kert as their protector from the usual Soviet Army bullying and humiliation. In the late 1980s, when the power of the Soviet Union started to show its first cracks, Kert returned to Estonia and joined forces with the independence movement.

"We started doing cybersecurity cooperation with their guard unit. They just wanted to do hands-on exercises and see what their attacks would look like," Evans said. "We created a massive exercise for their presidential office, all of their industry offices. From there, we gave them an introduction to the Cybersecurity and Infrastructure Security Agency."

Later, Kert founded the NATO Cooperative Cyber Defence Centre of Excellence. But it was his personal skills that stood out for Evans. It wasn't just a case of shared military and security interests that drew the two men together. It was friendship. They spent time with each other, understanding each other, understanding their shared motives and values, and only then building those bridges between the United States and Estonia.

Leadership isn't just about telling people what to do. It's about building that kind of camaraderie, helping each other and helping a community of practice that goes both ways.

"We learned a lot from the Estonians about cybersecurity," Evans said. "Because they do things differently, it helped us see the gaps in our own work process."

What is fundamentally great leadership in the world of cybersecurity?

It's about recognizing the capacity and the capabilities of your team, despite what you come into work believing is important and is not.

It's about taking the time to experiment, iterate, and learn, and to support team experimentation and reflection at work.

It's about having the guts to recognize creative opportunism in times of crisis.

We have to stop closing ranks and start opening them up.

PART THREE

ENTERING THE FRAY

7

UNDERSTANDING THAT TRUST IS A CURRENCY

TASK FORCE PINEAPPLE was originally created to evacuate American citizens and military allies after the Taliban's takeover of Afghanistan in August 2021. Scott Mann, a retired Green Beret, had discovered that an Afghan commando with whom he had once served was receiving death threats from the Taliban for having served alongside SEAL Team Six.

Mann got his friend out of the country, but within a very short period of time Task Force Pineapple grew to include not only other foreign nationals, but also Afghan families, organizations, and even sports teams. An encrypted chat room was set up in which over fifty Task Force Pineapple members, including veterans and former intelligence officers, collaborated with US Special Forces and the US embassy, but even then, the team outgrew its original project constraints. Backchannel links to foreign affairs contacts in countries worldwide facilitated the movement of over a thousand people in the first two weeks of its operations.

Like the Underground Railroad during slavery in the US South, passengers with the golden ticket—a picture of yellow pineapples on a pink background—were passed through conductor safehouse checkpoints between Afghanistan and countries to its east until they reached safety. While time passed too quickly, Task Force Pineapple members worked through the night, sometimes days without sleeping, to help the most at-risk people escape. These included not only former collaborators with the West but also teachers, journalists, children, people with disabilities, and others who would be likely targets of the Taliban's control.

Kristen Farnum, who was mentioned earlier in this book, was one of Task Force Pineapple's members, and she learned a lot about what matters in a time of crisis from this project, lessons she's applied since to similar efforts in Ukraine.

"When things are just starting to hit the fan, trust is your only currency," Farnum says. "When you can't trust your government to save you, you have to trust the people around you. You have to know who you can trust so that you know how you're going to get out alive."

Farnum is right. Building trust between people and communities is a fundamental pillar of humanity. It's how we get things done. Even without a political conflict on the horizon, we place a high value on knowing who is on our side and how we can work together.

However, from the point of view of cybersecurity and even the internet itself, our fundamental trust in each other is eroding.

The difficulty in relying on people online is that, well, the entities with which we interact aren't actually people. On social networks, we don't know when we're chatting with bots, for example. We can't tell whether the article we've just read has been written with AI. We're not sure whether the news video we've just witnessed is a deepfake.

For example, research from Microsoft demonstrates the ability to produce near real-time, lifelike audio-driven talking faces.[1] Using a single portrait photo (your LinkedIn profile pic), a brief audio clip (company address or shareholder report) generates lip-audio synchronized video in 512x512 45fps with only a 170-millisecond delay. Imagine powering customer support with artificial but lifelike AI-generated representatives. Now consider a deepfake video or conference call with your boss instructing you to wire funds to a new account.

ALL OF US are experiencing growing distrust in institutions. In twenty out of the twenty-eight countries surveyed by the Edelman Trust Barometer, average trust in institutions is less than 50 percent.[2] But what's driving this loss of trust? Trust started dropping during the 2008 global financial crisis and has continued to decline as a result of rapid globalization and technological change, the effects of which have not been equally shared across society. Recent scandals involving social intermediaries like Facebook (rebranded Meta) and companies like Tesla have also fueled public distrust, safety fears, and privacy concerns. And another theme comes up repeatedly in our most recent global conversations: corruption, namely the abuse of public office for private gain. Corruption both feeds and is fed by the broader crisis of trust, which sustains a vicious circle that undermines our social cohesion.

Stefan Korshak, an American war correspondent who has lived and worked in Kyiv, Ukraine, for more than twenty years, agrees. He also believes that it's getting harder for the average person to trust, well, anyone.

"Over time, people don't trust the information they receive even though they need it," Korshak explains. "We still understand that there's such a thing as a reliable and an unreliable source, but, in the present day, there is no such thing as an absolutely reliable source. People are afraid that, maybe, they're being played. Maybe other people have an agenda of their own. Maybe they're just making a mistake. Trust is a currency."

Just like Korshak has seen his industry erode because of a lack of trust, the same is true for my own industry. That's why one of the top-of-the-line security framework architectures out there is called Zero Trust, so named by the National Institute of Standards and Technology, part of the US Department of Commerce. It's been named Zero Trust because it requires every user inside and outside of an organization to be authenticated, authorized, and continuously validated for security configuration and posture before being granted or keeping access to applications and data. It acts on the premise that no one can trust each other, and only the technology will save us.

But cybersecurity industry leaders like David Shipley think that's a problem.

"Zero Trust is the latest cult," he argues. "Organizations rely on human beings to cooperate and trust each other. Trust is a currency in business. And all of a sudden, we're taking trust out of the equation. How does that work in a human society?"

Farnum, Korshak, and Shipley are saying the same thing, literally using the same words. Trust is a currency, perhaps the most important one we have. And trust is incredibly important not only in the digital age, but because of it.

Trust is the difference between getting out of Afghanistan alive and being killed at the border. But it's also nuanced; it's subtle. It's the ability to understand the meaning of words and why they are important to understanding policies and politics. And it's indelibly linked to the choices we make when we create, share, and store data as well.

YOU WILL EXPERIENCE a cybersecurity event; this is a given. Learning from cyber and military intelligence leaders, we know that digital invasions are only going to escalate. If trust is the only currency that matters, your job as the leader of an organization is to build internal and external trust networks so that when the event happens, you'll have the ability to navigate a minefield with the right team in place.

As Bob Darling reminded me in our conversation, from a leadership perspective, trust is tied to accountability. If you're going to go through a ransomware attack, you don't want to have to try and win over your team's trust on the fly. You also don't want your stakeholders to mistrust your ability, your intentions, or your decision-making prowess. That's why you need to develop your ability to build trust from the start of your tenure, not after an infiltration has taken place.

Why is this important? Because the reality is that your employees don't trust you.

In a given week, employees spend an average of 47 hours at work in North America. They also spend an average of 7 hours a week commuting, more in major centers. That's roughly 54 hours, more or less, that employees spend with their jobs out of 112 waking hours, and that allocation of time dedicated to work is only increasing.[3] That's half of employees' lives at or going to and from work. Add to this a disturbing survey result from the 2024 Gallup *State of the Global Workplace* report that suggests that 58 percent of people say they trust strangers more than their own boss. The same report tells us that, globally, 77 percent of employees are not engaged or are actively disengaged at work.[4]

Why do employees not trust their bosses? Demands on their time in the office are increasing, while the surveillance of day-to-day tasks is also on the up. The level of mental effort and strain that employees experience is consistently under-measured by companies. The same Gallup report says that

44 percent of employees said they experienced a lot of stress the previous day, repeating the record high in 2021 and continuing a trend of elevated stress that began almost a decade earlier. That may be why, according to Deloitte's 2024 workplace well-being survey, 71 percent of people in North America would walk right out the door and take a new job tomorrow if they were offered one.[5]

Trust, in the form of human connection at work, is nonexistent.

These employees are filling a seat and watching the clock. They put in the minimum effort required. Some employees even take actions that directly harm the organization, undercutting its goals and opposing its leaders. At some point along the way, the trust between employee and employer was severely broken.

Why?

Because there's a moment in every business school curriculum when a professor mentions Sun Tzu's *The Art of War*.

More than 2,500 years ago, the Chinese master strategist wrote this book about navigating through battle successfully, the first tenet of which is that you must know the enemy and yourself. Although originally meant to offer wisdom for generals, this principle is taught to upcoming business leaders as they sit in their desks in classrooms from Switzerland to Hong Kong to the United States as relevant to today's global business because it reads like a how-to for a multinational consumer products company: "The elements of the art of war are first, measurement of space; second, estimation of quantities; third, calculations; fourth, comparisons; and fifth, chances of victory."[6]

Professors argue that market competition is like a never-ending war and that we can use this text to gather, analyze, synthesize, and use information to make better decisions and take better actions on the field of play.

Business is a military hierarchy, and, traditionally, employees are expendable pawns on the front lines. It makes sense. Most of what we've created in the modern business world is a result of the post–World War II era: we created teams on the battlefield that we moved right into the boardroom when peace broke out.

But what happens when people are pawns, when they know that their interests are tertiary, their jobs precarious, their ideas subject to the hierarchy within the walls of their company? Competition. No matter how we try to sugarcoat it and tell people they are "teams of rivals" or "equals" or "peers" who mentor each other, most employees know on some level that this is not true. Not only are they required to compete against their similarly titled associates from other firms, but they usually compete for resources, managers' time, recognition, pay, and job security inside their own firm every single day.

Employees overcompensate and overcorrect because their journey at work is a solitary one. In fact, businesses worry that employees spend over eighty minutes a week in social conversation, as if this should be of deep concern.[7] Eighty minutes talking to each other weekly is perceived as bad. The characters that employees are asked to play run parallel to those of soldiers, disconnected from the ability to share human emotion at work, even if there are missions and value statements that superficially support teamwork. We all know that employees are told over and over again through sports and military metaphors that they are part of a team, that they have to follow a strategic plan linked to these metaphors.

So what happens when you have a workforce that doesn't want to be there and doesn't care about whether their work is any good? From the point of view of cybersecurity, you've just upped your risk by a million percent. No matter what Zero Trust products you have installed, you're screwed. And you're the one who is accountable.

The cybersecurity trope
PEBCAK—Problem Exists
Between Chair and Keyboard—
blames the individual.
It's the exact opposite.

TRUST, IN ALL DIRECTIONS, is a lost art that ought to count in our modern world because of the way it empowers an organization, both individually and together. Trust creates the desire, motivation, and will to work as a team that you can't build through a hierarchical, tightly controlled technological system. When trust increases in an organization, the degree of information sharing and work process outputs increases. And creating a culture of trust is associated with longer job tenure, greater job satisfaction, less chronic stress among employees, and higher productivity.[8]

I would argue that, in order to step away from being characters, we have to stop building teams and start building communities that center on trust. Businesses are not the army corps. CEOs are not generals. No lives are actually at stake when we sell a mobile phone or a pizza. In fact, nothing actually happens because a "company" or "team" does anything at all. Achievements take place because *people* achieve.

Yet a cybersecurity trope known as PEBCAK—in other words, the Problem Exists Between Chair and Keyboard—blames the individual. It's the exact opposite.

Individuals achieve. Individuals choose and change and innovate. If enough people are aligned and part of a community, change can be incredibly powerful. But if people are regimented into factions, competing, and are expected to march with precision every day, changes are constrained.

Building trust needs to start with coming to terms with your risks and feeling like you can trust yourself, Ed Schein, a former professor at the Massachusetts Institute of Technology Sloan School of Management, taught his students. The subject of Schein's lifelong research was organizational culture. Schein taught that trust at work evolves from dialogue with team members but that our own self-awareness is critical to making sure that dialogue is actually effective. In other words, if we understand our own motivations and speak from a place of authenticity, people will trust us more. If our only motivation as leaders is to impose our power on others and try to control them, we will fail.

The short version of this, as Jerry Colonna, the author of *Reboot: Leadership and the Art of Growing Up*, suggests, is that better humans make better leaders. So, to create more trust, you have to start by putting yourself through your paces.

"For several years, I trained our defense advisors going to Afghanistan," Farnum says, "and that included academic training, cultural training, and simulation training. On-site, we're blowing them up, and then we're breaking them down psychologically."

What Farnum describes isn't far off from what cybersecurity consultants will recommend. Understanding what might happen through tabletop simulation training is a start. Tabletop exercises and fire drills provide a forum in which team members can practice their roles and develop their deliverables. To simulate stress, offer rewards to encourage personal performance, or introduce changes, like the unavailability of key team members or guidance from senior leadership. Practice and training reinforce expectations and functions within the team and will likely expose concerns or ego-driven actions that can affect the outcome. They also expose the need for multiple modes of information transfer, group decision-making, and even bias toward specific notions or outcomes.

But understanding your own limitations and breaking out of overconfidence is just as important as tabletop exercises. As a leader, your opinion is important, but it's not the only opinion that will count if you face an attack.

Think about it this way. That Underground Railroad Farnum and her colleagues were engineering out of Afghanistan, constantly changing routes and communications standards, wouldn't have worked if that team of security experts hadn't all contributed their specialist insight. The same is true for your organization, unique in its own needs and resources, in the wake of a cybersecurity attack. If you get a grip on just how much support you'll need from your team in a crisis by anticipating a worst-case scenario, then you'll be creating the right mindset for building the trust you need within your organization. Only then can you begin to reach out for the help you will need on every level.

And you will need that help. It's not just your digital files that will need protecting or reconfiguring during an attack. You're going to need communications and public relations working overtime. Your customer service team will be on their phones with brand new information, and managers will need to be on top of every extra question. Depending on your business model, you may need to shut down or ramp up production or move it to a different location. You'll have legal on the line, especially if your customer or employee data is breached. Assistants will be running around. Food will need to be ordered in for employees who are doing the most. Human resources will have to reschedule holidays and pay for overtime or arrange comp days, depending on your legal obligations. Recall Darling's observation of a senior administrator like Condoleezza Rice, willing to get water for those working hard to protect the nation.

Given all of this responsibility, to build trust, you have to create technical, psychological, and social safety nets for all of your employees before, during, and after a crisis.

Instead of relying on top-down decisions alone, leaders should recognize the value in working together to lead changes and idea generation in a crisis collectively. Part of this is embracing polarizing points of view. When we're building trust, we can't simply ask employees to replicate management ideals. The people we want on board in a crisis are those who challenge each other to find better, faster, and more innovative solutions.

It's critical to ask for what you want, rather than how you want it done. As Darling puts it, "Give them the *what* and not the *how.*" To enhance trust, leaders need to allow employees to more fully manage their own work and their relationships within the organization. Self-management allows employees to work together in mutually efficient groups rather than be beholden to top-down oversight. High levels of autonomy have been found to correlate with great efficiency and high levels of personal motivation, according to psychologists Edward Deci and Richard Ryan.[9] People want to feel that they have an impact, and they need freedom of action to make this work. But to do this well, organizational priorities must be clear, well defined, transparent, and well communicated.

In addition, authority needs to be informal and based on honing one's ability to make connections, persuade, and motivate others. In order to create trusting relationships, leaders need to see, understand, and empathize with others, be they colleagues, employees, or any other stakeholders. Leaders must have the courage to commit themselves fully but also ask for support.

As a leader, if you want to address an unsolved issue in the workplace, dare to create a dialogue space. This requires at least one person to hold space for uncertainty and invite people to offer their insights, viewpoints, and experiences regarding the issue, even if uncomfortable ideas arise. Allowing for uncertainty requires the ability to share our perspective but then to put it aside and create space to listen deeply with an open mind, open heart, and open will, enabling new and creative ideas to emerge.

Leaders need to create trust within themselves, show up authentically, and be vulnerable. Trust in the workplace and within ourselves is important, but few understand what this means.

When we trust, our intuition, thoughts, and outer actions are in accord.

The same is true for organizations as it was for Task Force Pineapple: we have to trust our own instincts, and we have to trust those of others. We need to trust ourselves differently than we have in the past so that, in a crisis, we can collectively fly without a net.

8

ESTABLISHING CREDIBILITY

SOHO ROUTERS are a staple networking appliance for billions of consumers around the world. They are often the single point of data movement through a network, managing domain name resolution, firewall protections, dynamic addressing, wireless connectivity, and, of course, routing. In 2018, researchers reported that more than 500,000 SOHO routers in the United States were compromised by sophisticated Russian malware dubbed VPNFilter.

While that problem was fixed, it seemed to trigger a cascade of copycat problems.

By 2021, the Chinese hackers were found to be compromising both internet-facing DVR and IP cameras for use as command-and-control nodes through the installation of malware, and then used the botnet to target power grids in India. The US Cybersecurity and Infrastructure Security Agency (CISA) found the same thing happening stateside in 2022, noting that the Chinese were establishing persistent access into critical networks as a means of not only carrying out espionage but also preparing for targeted attacks on American power supplies.[1]

With the threat landscape changing so quickly, Lisa Plaggemier, the executive director of the National Cybersecurity Alliance, suggests there is a lot that we simply don't know and can't predict, even at the highest levels of security governance in the West. In addition, in her work at her nonprofit organization, dedicated to protecting people and organizations from cybercrime, she has witnessed a lot of misunderstanding and disbelief among organizational leaders because we're just not seeing these all-too-common breaches in the headlines.

"The Chinese did get into the US power grid. But it wasn't until some industry leaders testified before Congress and recounted those stories that the story was covered in the evening news. And there were just snippets of information, which I think is all anybody consumes anymore, unfortunately. In fact, I don't think the media even pointed out that the Chinese were in our power grid. The average American was exploited, and it wasn't just unpatched routers. It was everything that people were hooking up to them. One citizen's data was breached through an internet-connected dog collar."

The scope and scale of this grid hack are critical to understanding our current situation. Why was this not front-page news? Why are you only learning about this right now? Why are reports on this hack, even to this day, difficult to find in the mainstream media? In fact, because similar but different hacks are likely taking place right now, why aren't we being alerted to how we can prevent them in our own homes and offices?

"The reality of this situation is that it's akin to a soldier from the Chinese Communist Party standing in your living room," Plaggemier explains. "While this crossed the line into national security, it's the average person who is playing an unwitting role."

There has to be a disconnect here. The total lack of interest in this story, the story that the media completely missed, is critical for our personal and collective security. It affects families and organizations alike. So why are news agencies burying their heads in the sand?

"Maybe people don't want to hear it because it actually involves them having some responsibility to take care of the equipment that they purchase and bring into their home," Plaggemier suggests. "They set it and forget it. But we have to tell the story that nobody's talking about, because without real solutions, it leaves people with a feeling of helplessness. In fact, the news reinforces this misconception daily. We're witnessing apathy and surrender right out of the gate."

What's true for consumers is also true for organizational leaders. Because of the inevitability of cybersecurity breaches, many leaders choose to set it and forget it as well.

But shrugging off the Chinese Communist Party isn't leadership.

THE DUNNING-KRUGER EFFECT is rampant when it comes to IT.

What's the Dunning-Kruger effect? It's the idea that most people tend to overestimate their own level of knowledge and, as a result, struggle to accurately assess why things go wrong.[2] Applied to IT, Dunning-Kruger suggests that unless you come from a security background, you don't know what you don't know, especially at the leadership level. It even applies to experts. David Shipley calls the modern-day large language model, or AI, a Dunning-Kruger machine because only super-experts understand if it's actually lying to them.

But the fact is that information has gotten complicated and complex, and not just when it comes to trusting the news we read and watch. Since the 1970s, media trends have been connected to rapid social changes. Not only have we learned, as a global society, to increasingly communicate through the use of technology, but also our use of media has been integrated into our lives on a minute-by-minute basis. This means that the way we perceive and understand social norms in relation to how we exchange and reproduce information has also changed. These changes are also affected by increasing links between the creation of social networks such as social media, globalized cultural norms and social influences, and economic activities. We've disengaged from our critical thinking skills because we can't take it anymore, and we are fearful about what we can trust about each other.

Even if this is the case, it's up to you to get informed because you don't know what you don't know. Not just once, but on the regular. It's a constantly shifting threat landscape. There is no set-and-forget when it comes to cybersecurity.

Leaders have to acquire a high information quotient, a cyber IQ, if they want their businesses to survive. You need to move beyond talking the talk and really commit to building your IQ so that you can make strategic decisions when they matter. The famous quote attributed to Heraclitus, "Change is the only constant in life," implies that change begins as soon as life exists and ends only when it no longer exists. Having skills that allow us to accept life's changes and events with awareness and consciousness is the foundation of resilience.

But there is a lot standing in the way of your IQ. Some of this has to do with Moore's Law and the philosophy that surrounds it.

Co-founder of Intel Corporation (a former employer of mine) and the semiconductor industry forecaster Gordon Moore once predicted that the number of transistors on a microchip would double every two years although, in the same time period, the cost of computers would be halved. The idea is based upon the fact that our technologically informed world is shifting at such

Leaders have to acquire a high information quotient, a cyber IQ, if they want their businesses to survive.

a pace that we're likely going to continue to build forward at what we call hyperscale: the ability to meet the demand for computing and technological change as needed. But what happens in hyperscale is that we learn quickly about what doesn't work as much as what does work, and we change our plans accordingly.

What we didn't plan for becomes our next plan. The future we think we have is never the future we actually have. And yet, collectively, we are afraid of change and the uncertainty of what we have in front of us.

With how much faster the future is coming and how much harder it is to predict, there's a lot of insecurity surrounding what we ought to be doing with our interests, bodies, jobs, and every decision we make. We often hope for the best but plan for the worst. Jared Diamond, the Pulitzer Prize–winning author, geographer, and acclaimed anthropologist, in *Collapse: How Societies Choose to Fail or Succeed*, tells us that there are whole countries that have collapsed as a result of their inability to adapt, in part based on their fixation on a fear of the future, so much so that changing conditions overwhelmed them.[3] We're also afraid of our own personal futures: right now, we don't know whether our jobs will, in fact, be taken by robots, and this is especially true for your employees.[4]

The worst part is this: fear paralyzes us when we can't see a viable next step.[5] It's so paralyzing that researchers are coming up with new ways to measure our fear of the future.

One such measurement, the Dark Future scale, was devised in 2019 because, given the immense level of fear we embody in today's rapidly changing world, prior to this assessment we had no way of understanding just how much.[6]

Why do we feel so unequipped to deal with the future, and why don't we develop a cyber IQ that actually works? Human beings are, in fact, oriented toward the future. It's always on our minds. And yet there is a lack of preparation for everything the future offers. That's because embedded in the human experience is the scenario of being thrown into a time and space with a gap out in front of us. There are constantly disappearing horizons that amount to moving targets that not only shift but become visible and invisible. The future contains variables that we're not privy to yet, and there's no playbook for it. The fact that a person is faced with an ambiguous space is inextricably linked with some fear of it, and that's a positive adaptive mechanism. People differ in their tendency to feel anxiety, and this fear is also situationally conditioned. A certain fear for the future mobilizes effort, gives vividness to our experiences, and enriches life. That's because whatever comes next in our lives is never a straight shot. Rarely do we get a corner office without unintentionally alienating some clients along the way. Very few of us make it to the big leagues without getting cut from a team at some point, even when we put in the practice. No one publishes a book without having written several painstakingly edited drafts.

But something else standing in the way of your IQ is bias.

Biased judgment and decision-making decrease the ability of an individual to consider all of the options open to them in order to benefit their work and, therefore, to take leadership from other people when it is advantageous.[7]

In my previous book, *No Safe Harbor: The Inside Truth About Cybercrime—and How to Protect Your Business*, I discussed human biases that rob us of the opportunity to uncover root cause and lead to outcomes that minimize impact to the business. As Sidney Dekker explains in his book *The Field Guide to Understanding "Human Error,"* we are skewed by our tendency to hindsight bias, our exaggerated belief that we would avoid a now understood event, and outcome bias, our tendency to demand that those at fault be held accountable. When I use the term judgment, I mean sound decision-making, not passing judgment and determining punishment.

It's important for us to consider alternative explanations than the ones in our own head, anchors we're carrying, possible outcomes, perspectives, and countervailing evidence, and to consider potential situational influences on our behavior, as well as the ability to balance perceived rules and options to change the status quo, but the reality is that we don't when we're constrained by a business ethos that rejects the fluidity and adaptability that comes naturally to us as people.

THEN, WE MUST challenge ourselves to go deeper into why we think the way we do, why we have biases, where our egos cause us to act. Confirmation bias, for example, is the human tendency to search for, interpret, favor, and recall information in a way that confirms or supports our prior beliefs or values. It's critical to reflect on our own potential for confirmation bias and overconfidence, allowing us to better differentiate between relevant and irrelevant information.

There's a behavioral change process called the Capability, Opportunity, Motivation, and Behavior (COM-B) model that's really helpful at getting to the heart of self-awareness.[8] It's a strategy tool for developing awareness of your own behaviors and, as a result, understanding how to change them to build your capacity for leveling up. While the COM-B model originated from health psychology, it has recently been applied to organizational behavior and is increasingly being used as a leadership tool. The model suggests that behaviors are influenced by three interconnected components: capability (the individual's psychological and physical capacity to engage in the activity concerned), opportunity (the factors that make the behavior possible or prompt it), and motivation (the processes that energize and direct behavior).

So what can you do with COM-B? Answer the following questions.

Capability. What are your capabilities? These include your knowledge, skills, and both physical and cognitive abilities. What capabilities do you need to lead in a cybersecurity emergency? What's the gap between the two lists? Consider how to develop the capabilities you need and where you're going to reach out for assistance.

Opportunity. The opportunity component refers to external factors that facilitate or hinder a particular behavior, including environmental factors, social norms, and physical and social opportunities required to perform or change behavior. What are your specific barriers to cybersecurity leadership excellence?

Motivation. The motivation component alludes to the cognitive and emotional processes that drive a particular behavior, integrating the conscious and unconscious factors influencing an individual's desire or willingness to engage in a behavior. What are the conscious factors getting in your way of building a team that will succeed in fighting cybercrime? Your personal values? Have a think about whether you might bring your unconscious biases to the surface.

Self-awareness is just this: we need to take the thoughts we have and see them through the following four practices every day, helping us to develop our IQ, especially with the world moving as fast as it is.

We should take it as a given that we don't know all the answers and seek them out. The world we live in today is nothing like the world you lived in when you got your first job. There is a future, even one five years from now, that we can't even imagine or fathom, if we believe what those who are tracking human progress, change, and challenge tell us. We should read and understand what we can from cybersecurity newsletters and websites, like those provided by governments and trusted sources like Hacker News, *Infosecurity Magazine,* and *Dark Reading.*

We need to break out of our expected hierarchical structure, norms, and rules to access organizational IQ. To be able to move as fast as the world around us does, we need to sit down with our IT teams and ask what we need to know now, perhaps even as much as twice per month.

We ought to build a practice around opening up the door to changing direction. We need to make the kind of everyday decisions that allow us to adapt. These decisions don't have to be large, mind-bending ones in order to help us move toward security. Each of us needs to keep changing so that we can reinvent our organizational futures with everything that we continually learn.

We need the mental space to make IQ a priority. Each of us has to cultivate the desire to embrace change and truly love the radically possible, rather than leaning back on what's been done before. We must put effort into what we have learned, and become more content and more successful doing things the IQ way, rather than simply following the script we wrote for ourselves years ago. We can build more awareness of how we are using our IQ and how we can continue to grow and evolve our organizations as a result.

9

BEING ACCOUNTABLE

"IMAGINE THE car industry," James Lin said to me one day. "What if, when a company engineers a car, they decide to make random changes to familiar designs. Say, if you buy a Ford the brake is on the left, and if you buy a GM the brake is on the right."

"Sure," I responded. "For the consumer, that would be crazy. You'd have accidents all over the place."

"Now, apply the same idea to the software industry," Lin continued. "Because that's exactly how the software industry operates. For every piece of software, industry vendors come up with their own standards. Why? Because confusing the consumer, and especially the business consumer, makes them money."

I thought about what he was saying, and I knew he was making sense.

One company I worked with years ago got a call from Microsoft because they were beyond their billing band. Their storage capacity and traffic volume were higher than the license tier they had paid for. Why? Their Office 365 account had been taken over, and the hackers used their account as a drop box. Hackers were dumping stolen content into it and then pulling it out. Microsoft didn't catch any part of that massive security breach, but their billing department wanted money for the activity. Microsoft's motivation wasn't security; it was their revenue stream. And they were willing to bill their client for the hacking activity taking place within their software.

They didn't know, and no one flagged it on the side of the internet service provider (ISP) either. The ISP should have noticed the spike in traffic on their own. There was no consistency across software, no easy way to see these spikes, and as a result, there was no accountability.

Perhaps worse, in other words, no one wanted to take responsibility for what was happening.

"While things have changed in the last few years since that breach took place, we're still not seeing the kind of standards that we need in place in our industry. Cybersecurity needs car-industry-level standards," Lin notes.

Lin is right. We need those kinds of standards so that leaders can make decisions more easily, find information more quickly, and ensure a high level of accountability. But the reality is that there are significant standards gaps that aren't going to be rectified soon.

Without standards and regulations that force companies to adopt them, the onus for accountability is on leaders.

The scope and scale of digital invasions at present means that the FBI, the police, and the CIA are not coming to save you. As I've already explained, these and other crimefighting agencies simply don't have the human resources to ensure that every digital crime is prosecuted. And minimum mandatory controls in your IT systems are only a baseline defense because of the standards gaps that Lin and other cybersecurity experts identify every day.

Even so, you are the last line of accountability for cyber-crime. Your board or shareholders are not going to take "I just didn't know" for an answer.

AS A LEADER, you need to be accountable to your stakeholders without expecting to lean on government support systems. This is true whether you're facing a ransom of $500 or $50 million. If you aren't accountable, those hands-off governments are going to make you accountable.

In the United Kingdom, right now, new legislation is coming that will mandate all organizations to report ransomware attacks to the government.[1] On top of this, the legislation will require all victims to seek a license before making any extortion payments.

On the surface, it sounds like a great idea.

British officials believe the mandatory reporting require-ment would help illuminate the true scale of the problem. And, included in this legislation is a complete ban on ransom payments for organizations involved with critical national infra-structure, like transportation companies and hospitals. The ban intends to remove the incentive for hackers to disrupt these critical services by preventing them from monetizing attacks.

Behind the scenes, the UK's National Cyber Security Cen-tre and the Information Commissioner's Office have expressed concern that ransomware victims were keeping incidents secret, which is indeed the case. Many organizations without public responsibilities, such as private companies, don't share their cybercrime incidents at the risk of alarming their stake-holders, hoping they can simply pay off criminals and make the problem go away. If, however, governments make this ille-gal, then victims of ransomware attacks won't be able to hide their payments any longer. At the same time, there is a risk that the application process could delay recovery and poten-tially increase the harm and disruption caused by a ransom-ware attack.

You are the last line
of accountability. Your
shareholders are not going
to take "I didn't know"
for an answer.

While it's not yet clear how the licensing regime would work in the UK as the legislation is still going through public consultation, it's evident that a version of this kind of mandatory reporting is likely going to become a new norm. When it comes to massive ransom demands, our legislators have been missing in action for a long time, so any shift in the status quo is likely to shake things up for the better. If new legislative ideas prompt debate, that's going to be helpful.

In late 2023, the US government fired the first personal accountability shot across the bow of corporate America when the Securities and Exchange Commission (SEC) filed charges against Tim Brown, then CISO of SolarWinds, including fraud and internal control failures.[2] The charges stem from an investigation of the 2020 SUNBURST attack against SolarWinds, a $3 billion technology management firm. This is the first (known) case of a government agency naming individuals and charging them based on evidence in the form of board reports, lectures, and public announcements.

These new ideas and potential legal jeopardies also should prompt new levels of accountability. Whether or not mandates exist, hiding from stakeholders will not serve your organization.

Think about it this way: Nature abhors a vacuum, right? Something's going to rush in to fill the blank space. With cybersecurity, I think that's exactly what happens.

If you have a dysfunctional organization, you create a gap that can be filled.

If you don't communicate clearly and concisely to your stakeholders, that's another gap.

If you have high turnover, that's a huge knowledge retention gap at your organization.

If you don't make a commitment to your IT team, you're creating another gap.

In my work as a cybersecurity consultant, I've noticed that many leaders don't want to take accountability. If things are going well, leaders take credit. If they aren't, leaders will blame their IT team or the person who clicked on the phishing link, even if they had no training systems in place.

A lot of this lack of accountability comes back to habits. But if your fallback relies on your habits, the way you navigate your known knowns rather than your unknown unknowns, you will fail.

Over the last decade, the business and personal growth best-seller lists in the Western world have been filled with books on taking advantage of that human compunction for creating and maintaining good habits. Although it could be said that this trend began decades earlier with the seminal book by Stephen Covey, *The 7 Habits of Highly Effective People*, in recent years we have been inundated with Charles Duhigg's *The Power of Habit*, James Clear's *Atomic Habits*, Richard O'Connor's *Rewire*, Gretchen Rubin's *Better Than Before*, and the list goes on. In all of these books, the message is very simple: find a way to do better things (rather than worse things) repeatedly, and you'll be successful, happy, and wise.

But habits aren't strategic.

First of all, habits are largely based on social signals, not on human behaviors. In the brain, habits are very much tied to that Pavlovian dog response that we've all read about hundreds of times.[3] In other words, creating habits is deeply tied to value-based decision-making in which we value a kind of behavior, repeat it so that we fit in, and value ourselves for being like other people. Scientists even say that social norms, namely the things that absolutely everyone does, such as following traffic signal laws, are a kind of super-habit. Having a habit, therefore, is very much like mastering basic childlike behavior. It's not about going above and beyond and becoming super successful.

Because habits are social, we can also be readily influenced by those around us in more ways than one. Addiction is a habit, for example. We become addicted to things and activities because of the way they make us feel and because they trigger patterns in our brains that allow us to calm ourselves. That's why researchers also think that acute or chronic stress can increase people's reliance on habits, and that habits are a coping mechanism to deal with painful challenges in life.[4] As well, as habits strengthen, they gradually become independent of our understanding of why we do the things we do. Even when habits don't serve us, we keep on keeping on because of the motor memory we have in our brains.

And then, because we have habits, many of us stop resolving our own problems because we've got a system in place that we think is working.[5] We lean back on what we've practiced as habits, and we don't continue to change it up based on new information. In fact, almost 50 percent of what we do on a daily basis at work is simply habit.[6]

Habits represent safe ways of protecting our egos and our psyches from the stresses of daily life, but they aren't going to make our world, businesses, and selves better. We take it as a given that the world we live in today is nothing like the world we lived in decades ago. We need to break out of structure, of norms, of rules, and we need to be able to move as fast as the world around us does. We need to change our attitude about our responsibility to keep up. What we must do is build a practice around opening up the door to the kind of everyday decisions that can change our ability to adapt and let go of the fear of change. On this path, we can shape the workplace of the future, one that is inevitably changing every moment.

To take true accountability and be a true leader, you have to create a deliberative space for best practices. You have to set aside superficial accountability to build a safer and more secure organization. You have to commit to becoming universally accountable for your organization and your choices. You must understand that your team's best effort depends on your ability to use best practices rather than rely on your old habits. You must hold the line, if only because governments, justice agencies, and software providers will not.

Let's take the example of Indigo Books, Canada's biggest bookseller.

As of the time of writing, Indigo is still recovering from a cyberattack that downed its website for a lengthy period in 2023. The attack has been connected to a series of quarterly losses leading up to a January 2024 layoff and a succession of changes that saw four of ten board members depart in 2023 due to a loss of confidence in board leadership.

As a long-tail result of the infiltration at Indigo, shareholders voted to approve a deal that saw the retailer become a private company in May 2024. According to Indigo's founder, Heather Reisman, this was the only way Indigo would be able to undertake a necessary transformation strategy.

"The rationale is not to be saddled with public reporting responsibilities because Indigo has been through a lot," said Richard Leblanc, a professor of governance, law, and ethics at York University in Toronto, in February 2024, when the Trilogy firms made their offer. To this end, the privatization would allow the company to avoid some scrutiny as it works to bring profitability and growth back to the bookstore chain.[7]

In this case, one could argue that Indigo took accountability for their cyberattack in the best way they knew how. Reisman's spouse, Gerald Schwartz, owns the company that bought back Indigo from shareholders, taking responsibility for the loss and ensuring that shareholders did not lose out financially. In that way, Reisman and Schwartz were accountable. But not every organization has an angel to step in and whisk away the debris of such an attack.

Another example is the MGM Grand casino and resorts chain in Las Vegas. In September 2023, guests reported issues with slot machines, ATMs, digital key cards, electronic payments, and online reservations. Ironically, the attack started in August during the cybersecurity conference Black Hat. While staying at the Luxor (part of the MGM family), I didn't use the app to book and check in. Scattered Spider and BlackCat/ALPHV ransomware gangs took responsibility for the attack, which started with a call to MGM's third-party help desk to phish credentials.[8] The attack was clever in its sophistication, but MGM responded and was up and running in weeks. They were prepared, had plans in place, and practiced attacks like this one. They knew the risks and were prepared to face them.

A better approach has to anticipate change and even embrace it.

Think of Bob Johansen and inverting VUCA to identify dysfunction in the face of uncontrolled circumstances, discussed in Chapter 3.

Every seven years every cell in our body is replaced. Our brains are constantly changing as we grow and learn, building new neural pathways. When we learn ideas or acquire new knowledge, we're developing new perspectives on the world around us. Our working communities and business strategies come and go because sometimes we change in a way that allows for success, and sometimes change separates us from our goals. Either way, we're becoming new versions of ourselves every day.

And yet if we're afraid of change, of knowing that next is always just over the hill that never ends, then we're not going to become advocates for what is best for our organizations.

So, ask yourself these core questions. This is where you practice a deep dive into accountability. These questions allow you to build the capacity for adapting to an uncertain security future so that you can take accountability in a way that will actually change the outcome during a cybersecurity event.

1 **Where are there dysfunctions in your organization?** Think about absolutely everything that could be defined as an accountability gap at work. You already know those little challenges in the organization that keep popping up, that you keep thinking about. The things that just are not aligned. You may have been planning to make some changes to address these gaps, but you just haven't found the time because they require an overwhelming amount of work. It could be anything: low morale, high turnover, so-called personality conflicts (which are usually not actual personality conflicts but management failures). Focus on one issue.

2 **What do you think you should be doing about this issue?** Write down what you would normally be doing to address the gap you're witnessing. Does your solution involve passing on the work to someone else? Convincing yourself that it isn't really a problem? Ask yourself why.

3 **Why haven't you addressed this issue yet?** Reflect on why you've not followed your own best practices. Not enough time, money, or support is usually the answer to this question, but dig deeper. Ask yourself the most uncomfortable questions right now. What aren't you admitting to yourself? How does taking this on and being truly accountable for the outcome feel? What would it feel like if you did take on this accountability and got it wrong? What would it feel like if you did take on this accountability and got it right?

4 **Can you find an innovative solution based on evidence?** Literally none of us has enough time, money, or support to do everything perfectly. Remember, we're humans, not robots, and we're flawed. And those flaws make us adaptable and unique, so we're never going to create a solution that will fit perfectly, or orchestrate a strategy where everything is

just going to happen naturally. So, where can you find new solutions from outside of your own wheelhouse? No, I don't mean by calling a consultant or accountant. I mean asking people within your organization, taking a course, reading high-level peer-reviewed research, or combining all of these ideas to carefully look at your options.

5 **What is the first thing you can do to start to address this problem?** I'm not asking you to do everything at once or magic your way into a solid solution. Start with thinking about the next step you can take toward accountability, realistically and immediately.

6 **How can you evaluate your first steps?** You're not alone in this process. You need to vet your ideas as you proceed, and you need buy-in from your stakeholders. Take an active role in evaluating what you do, early and often.

Let's face it. As a leader, you know how to do a lot of these things already. The challenge is that, as leaders, we often tell ourselves that we don't have the time to really dig into entrenched issues and dysfunctions. Except we already use big, scary, intangible words like "exponential change," "speed," "disruption," and "innovation" in our organizational strategies. As leaders, we have to allow for the unpredictable, the possibility of chaos that is the future of the modern workplace, to become an opportunity rather than a burden.

Recognize your power to advocate for change. Legitimate power is associated with occupying a position of authority. This includes the ability to set budgets, decide who to hire, set performance targets, provide or withhold rewards, and hold people accountable. Expert power is that associated with being a subject matter or process expert, with or without an educational designation. Both of these kinds of power are needed to facilitate universal accountability, and, as we've discussed in Chapter 8, you need a little of both if you're going to be successful at protecting your organization.

Take intentional action. Be clear on what that action is that you need to take, but build out your intentions first. What does it mean to be intentional? Just what it sounds like: It's about asking yourself questions about why things are happening, on purpose, before you lead. It's digging into what actually matters rather than relying on old organizational norms and habits.

Focus on possibility rather than fear. Leading from the realm of possibility is a process of learning to adjust to every new opportunity and barrier that the future throws at us. It's building in the possibility to adapt, revise, and recalibrate.

Take ownership. When something goes wrong, or when you don't understand what's at stake or even what's happening, check yourself first. Be proactively transparent about when you're not perfect. It allows others to not be perfect too, so that instead of hiding mistakes, we own up to them and move on.

We have to be advocates for our needs when it comes to the security of our organizations. This means that we have to have a high enough cyber IQ to engage in what's going on at the legislative and criminal justice levels, so that we can create the right balance between accountability to our organizational stakeholders and to society. If not for the greater good. The SEC is changing the meaning of ROI from "return on investment" to "risk of incarceration."

We must use our power as leaders to seek solutions before our security problems become too big to fix. We must embrace accountability so that we can take steps to address dysfunction early and often.

10

EMPOWERING PEOPLE

UNITEDHEALTH GROUP, founded in 1977, is an American-based multinational health insurance and services company based in Minnetonka, Minnesota. It sells insurance products under UnitedHealthcare, and under the trade name Optum it sells health care services and care delivery aided by technology and data.

Globally, UnitedHealth is the eleventh-largest company by revenue and the largest health care company by revenue.

In 2024, UnitedHealth Group CEO Andrew Witty faced a barrage of questions during a US Senate hearing into the company's response to a $22 million ransom demand from BlackCat/ALPHV. Witty admitted that maybe a third of all Americans' personal data had been affected by the breach. He blamed the attack on the fact that one of its subsidiaries stored patient data both on premises in data centers and in the cloud and had failed to install the proper multifactor authentication protocols.

Witty also admitted that he made the decision to pay the ransom without informing the US government.

Perhaps even worse, UnitedHealth Group did not take accountability for what the US Senate and House of Representatives, including both Republicans and Democrats, are suggesting is massively damaging to the health care industry as a whole.

Why? The breach has led to not only a massive amount of costly software changes across the entire industry but also a backlog of claims from both medical organizations and patients, meaning that Medicare itself, the backbone of the US health care system, is hurting. Much of the information in the restored systems is inaccurate or missing data, complicating processes further for all stakeholders and making everyday health care paperwork impossible. On top of all of this, UnitedHealth Group was accused of using this breach as a means of purchasing health care organizations it had burdened with this nightmare at pennies on the dollar.[1]

It could be argued that Witty, like so many CEOs before him, simply looked for a financial win (or the lesser of two evils) in a terrible situation. To do that, however, he may have had to let go of any semblance of accountability to anyone other than his shareholders, according to the senators now at his heels and subjecting him to ongoing interviews. His choice is certainly bold in the wake of such extreme havoc. The BlackCat/ALPHV cybersecurity threat is over for the time being. The impact of UnitedHealth Group's choices, however, are likely to result in waves of negative impacts for years, if not decades, to come.

In this respect, cyberattacks have long tentacles. They don't just affect organizations in terms of financial and data security loss. These attacks can have carry-on effects with respect to business strategy, customer viability, and service provision.

When these carry-on effects result in decisions that enhance problems for individual business units, that's not smart. Sure, UnitedHealth Group is allowed to make money in whatever way they want, but after their attack they distanced themselves from their teams on purpose. They left their subsidiaries and their employees hanging. Instead of finding collective solutions and leaning into their strategic human resources, UnitedHealth Group alienated non-shareholder stakeholders across the board. Employees, unit and subsidiary leaders, patients, and governments—all have been left wondering what to do and what went wrong.

The threat of cyberattacks fundamentally disrupting essential services like health care is one of the foremost concerns of governments around the world. This UnitedHealth Group attack was not only important in terms of its size, but also what lessons it imparts about the potential effects of other kinds of attacks. Yes, cyberattacks could significantly impact clinics' and hospitals' collective ability to provide essential services. But interruptions to essential services such as internet, electricity, transportation, water, and food supply systems are likely to become more and more common due to regular cyberattacks, disrupting everyday life as well.

Breaches aren't just about organizations. They are about all of us. Everything that we rely upon in this world can and will be disrupted by cybercrime. That is why every person to whom you owe a legal and financial responsibility, and especially your employees, ought to be empowered to take part in the prevention of cybercrimes.

LET'S LOOK AT the big picture for a second.

In 1970, the Chicago School economist Milton Friedman stated that the only social responsibility of business is to increase profits, and that the more money businesses make, the more social good will prevail. Businesses, he said at the time, shouldn't bother donating money to charities.[2]

It was a pretty simple argument, at least in Friedman's mind. If businesses were to contribute to social charitable works or social services, they would be, in effect, imposing taxes on themselves. This would be the case even if business leaders decided how these proceeds ought to be spent.

Friedman didn't want anything disrupting the work of Adam Smith's "invisible hand" behind the market. His ideas were similar to the well-disputed theory of trickle-down economics, in which the more money a business made, the more people they'd be able to employ. The faster that money changed hands, Friedman stated, the more possible it would be to employ more people at a higher wage rate, and the more money those people would be able to spend on goods and services. In theory, this idea would increase the rate of growth within a country, society as a whole would be better off, and no charities would be needed.

He meant well. Friedman argued for a focus on personal and corporate gain because he recognized it would be in an individual's best interest to ensure their society is also safe, secure, and growing in a profitable manner.

But Friedman forgot about a couple of things. First, he underestimated the Machiavellian instincts of the average business leader in their boomer years, people like Witty. These people didn't think about the social impact of business. There's a reason Bret Easton Ellis wrote *American Psycho*: the role of self-interest in boomer extractive capitalism was paramount, so much so that it became a satirical trope. Second, each business and each market is situated in a social context and is in fact part of our social world, whether leaders recognize this fact or not. It's more than a one-way economic relationship. Their services become integral to the fabric of the community and its constituents.

It has become clear in the last few decades, looking at the progression of factors leading to both the global economic crisis of 2008 and corporate fiascos spanning from the Enron affair to Theranos, that some business leaders felt they had both the right and the responsibility to make risky and unethical moves because their shareholders' earnings depended on them doing so, not unlike UnitedHealth Group. These are the kinds of business events that make the West a target for state cybercriminal actors. They also draw criticism within the West itself.

But the reality is that business does not operate in isolation, totally disconnected from other areas of life.

Here's an example of why that's the case: taxes. Thousands of headlines across the globe have touted the news that Jeff Bezos, one of the world's richest people, rarely, if ever, pays income tax, along with other American billionaires. Between 2014 and 2018, Jeff Bezos paid a true tax rate of 0.98 percent, Warren Buffett 0.1 percent, and Michael Bloomberg 1.3 percent, while the average American wage earner pays close to half their income in taxes, according to IRS data.[3] But these individuals' tax avoidance is dwarfed by multinational corporations' avoidance of taxation. Starbucks, for example, over a period of fifteen years of operations in the UK, was found to have paid UK corporate income taxes only once, and this was largely achieved through legal tax avoidance schemes.[4] That's why the G7 nations agreed to set a minimum global corporate tax rate of 15 percent to combat this problem in June 2021. But this decision is already facing challenges, as countries such as Switzerland and Singapore are looking for ways to support multinational corporations that want to bypass these taxation regimes.[5]

In other words, the tax revenue that was regularly collected in Friedman's heyday just isn't collected anymore. Most importantly, that's billions upon billions of dollars in tax revenue that could have been used to develop strong international crimefighting units to enforce cybersecurity and prosecute criminals.

Before he died, Friedman recanted his view that the only focus of businesses should be profit.[6] His argument, he said, was actually suggesting that ethical leadership ought to include sustainable leadership and business practices, but that's not how it was interpreted. It was interpreted in the least kind, least human way.

It's important to do things differently if we want to fight cybercrime. For us to work effectively, we have to work to support social good. And to do this, the organizational loopholes that alienate stakeholders have to be closed.

AS A LEADER with a cybersecurity responsibility, creating internal social support systems is critical to your strategy. Healthy social support systems start with empowered employees.

Employees' empowerment is linked to their sense of contribution, not their fundamental role or place in the organizational chart. Being respected for who they are, rather than what you want them to do, is critical to their sense of accomplishment. That's why, in 2024, the American Psychological Association said that 93 percent of workers want to be reminded that their work has purpose and meaning outside of a paycheck.[7]

Without a sense of meaning, workplace satisfaction erodes and employees tap out of their interest in helping their employer achieve goals. This is especially the case for goals that are not aligned with their day-to-day job role; for employees who have no direct responsibility or training in cybersecurity, there is no incentive to pay attention. But often, the response by businesses to workplace dissatisfaction is somewhat ludicrous. Much has been written about ping-pong-table cultures, where organizational leaders bring in games, free kombucha, and stand-up desks to increase workplace satisfaction. What

Giving people space, freedom, and permission to make more intentional decisions allows for organizations to succeed in extreme crisis situations.

actually ends up happening in those offices is that workplace satisfaction goes up by exactly zero percent. Ping-pong tables aren't really a good solution for building capacity in a company. The real answer is to facilitate true empowerment.

What does true empowerment look like? When the world becomes faster and burdened by more complexity and constraints than ever before, giving people space, freedom, and permission to make more intentional decisions not only allows them to succeed, but it also allows for organizations to succeed in extreme crisis situations.

More than anything, you need to provide employees with training, practice, and testing for the fight ahead. Your people, in almost every department in your organization, will matter most in the event of an attack. Any communication vacuum will be filled with misinformation, so you need a team that is prepared to take action under their own direction even when there are rapidly moving targets in place.

Ask more questions, every day. An effective leader questions standard procedures and processes to create an environment for new thinking to emerge. This provides a powerful counterpoint to the assumption that one leader alone has the ability to negotiate organizational change and build capacity among their team members.

Get your junior people, especially those in critical roles like communication and human resources, to conduct tabletop exercises. Practice makes perfect. These exercises show them their value in crisis and how important they are to the organization. You need to elevate and empower your employees. This goes beyond telling people that they have the power to make changes. Your employees have to *know* they have power. Each team member should be assessed for their own abilities, and work ought to be delegated to provide opportunities for growth and development.

Expand your inner circle. The normal tiers of command go from C-suite and director roles, down to managers, and then down to employees. Look at how you can organize people differently, bringing more people into the loop to build on your cyber IQ discoveries. If power is concentrated in only one individual or small group, then there is no possibility for innovation; capacity and empowerment need to be recognized as central to organizational development.

Make ethics a priority. A good leader exhibits trust and high moral standards. This is a person others view as powerful and want to emulate based on their morality versus their position. If people are empowered to engage in leadership at every level and believe in their ability to make a positive impact on the organization, this creates a foundation of mutual respect and positive engagement, shifting the focus of all individuals working on the same team toward collective achievement.

11

INVESTING WHERE
IT COUNTS

PLANE LANDED IN the Serbian capital of Belgrade in April 2020, a month into the lockdowns of the COVID-19 pandemic, bearing gifts.

It was, as we all know, a time of incipient fear. In places like Wuhan, New York City, and Rome, people were dying faster than authorities could bury them. When the People's Republic of China offered the world their newest invention, the Fire-Eye, a sophisticated portable lab that could detect coronavirus infections from leftover genetic fragments, the government of Serbia immediately put their hand up and asked for help.[1] The machine, which excelled at deciphering genetic instructions, was so helpful that Serbia turned its Fire-Eye lab into a permanent genetic research and data housing facility for studying viruses and understanding the scope of variability in the country's human DNA. The same pattern quickly repeated around the world. More than twenty countries also accepted offers of free Fire-Eyes, Canada, Latvia, Saudi Arabia, Ethiopia, South Africa, and Australia among them.

The fact is that human DNA data is a highly valuable commodity. The benefit of genetic testing is that new advances in the delivery of genome assemblies have made it possible for scientists to track and assess large-scale data, which may benefit society as it results in the creation of new fields for disease research. With advances in genetic coding and sequencing, there has been a rise in interest in genome data that can be used to predict the onset of diseases or even their prevention remedies. This requires assessing billions of combinations of factors, which may produce new and innovative medical knowledge that can contribute to care. As a result, there has been a global attempt to tap into new sources of human DNA around the world, since each newly generated solution could be a source of masses of novel streams of revenue.

The China National GeneBank is a government-owned genetic data repository that publicly aims to become the world's leader in biotechnology by 2035.[2] In doing so, it aims to gain an economic and strategic advantage over the United States.

China has undoubtedly used the Fire-Eye to collect this data. According to reporters at the *Washington Post*, they've admitted it publicly.

It's probably the reason that TikTok, owned by Beijing-based tech giant ByteDance, is being seen as a similar kind of Trojan horse. While US-founded companies Facebook, Instagram, Snapchat, and YouTube all collect similar amounts of data to TikTok, the worry is that TikTok could end up being a powerful weapon. There is always the possibility that the company could influence communication or other forms of infrastructure during times of conflict, likened to the similar US call to block Chinese telecom giant Huawei from being deployed in 5G infrastructure based on theoretical risks.

But are the risks that theoretical? Let's look at some examples.

In 2004, Nortel's fiber-optics equipment was the world's envy, with 70 percent of global internet traffic running off of this Canadian technology. But that year, a hacker infiltrated a Nortel server used to warehouse sensitive intellectual property through the accounts of at least seven Nortel executives.

Tracking the activity back to Shanghai, Nortel soon discovered that there was more to the hack than simple hacking. The hackers knew exactly what was happening within Nortel's board of directors, timing the extraction of a massive cache of records to exactly when they'd be caught up in meetings. Someone physically placed inside Nortel to commit espionage was creating an information siphon directly to China.[3]

Internally, Nortel cybersecurity advisor Brian Shields knew what was happening, but the C-suite didn't take his warnings seriously. In 2009, after the company had lost out on a series of contracts to China's state-champion company Huawei in which Huawei seemed to have replicated their technology, Nortel went bankrupt.

Something similar happened to Cisco. Cisco got out in front of a hack by Huawei and sued Huawei in 2003 over theft of designs and software code.[4] Huawei did admit to using a few lines of code, but Cisco claimed they had copied the entire design. In 2004, the suit was settled out of court, with no admission of guilt.

RICHARD STAYNINGS, currently chief security strategist for Cylera and a professor at the University of Denver, is a global expert in cybersecurity for health care and life sciences. He used to have a leading role at Cisco, and he knows a great deal about the kinds of risks we're talking about here.

Perhaps most importantly, Staynings knows just as much about China's capacity to create unpredictable risks for organizations. He has spent a large part of his career dealing with companies that have been the subject of Chinese cyberattacks.

"China is in a sustained multi-decade-long battle for world hegemony," Staynings says. "This is something that was actually in Mao's Little Red Book, or, to give its full title, *Quotations from Chairman Mao Zedong*, how China would dominate the world. Mao said that China could take advantage of the gullibility of the West. With our myopic four-year election and policy cycles, China has the capacity to beat us at our own game."

Given that mandate, Staynings suggests, it's almost impossible to overstate the risk that every organization faces.

"It's utterly incredible the lengths to which China goes to steal intellectual property and commercial trade secrets from the West," he told me. "We've seen these types of cyberespionage campaigns in many industries. In 2018, we discovered that the Supermicro motherboards that were being used in Congress included an extra substrate, a hidden chip, which was tracked to China. But the motherboards themselves were ostensibly manufactured by a Taiwanese company based in Silicon Valley that had offshored its manufacturing capabilities. The motherboards were also sold to Google and Apple, and they [Google and Apple] were able to track and identify extraneous traffic that was going back to China periodically and alerted the FBI."

If it weren't for Google and Apple, Staynings suggests, Congress might never have known what was taking place.

Staynings provides another salient example, and one that might be much more likely to take place in the average American organization. If you're leading an organization that wants to benefit from expansion into China, pay attention.

Staynings was consulting for a pharmaceutical company that had weathered a sustained attack by the Chinese state to exfiltrate all of their intellectual property, their commercial trade secrets. The fact is, however, that this attack was a result of the pharmaceutical company's planned expansion into the BRICS nations.

"One of the Chinese conditions of that expansion was that the pharmaceutical company had to partner with a local manufacturer of drugs in China, complete local research, and undertake local drug trialing," Staynings explained to me. "The rationale was that Chinese people are different from all other ethnicities, and they eat different foods, and they have different lifestyles, so the testing was warranted. But it was a veiled attempt to basically just steal the entire drug, drug profiling data, and clinical trial process."

In trying to be culturally competent and respectful, that pharmaceutical company literally gave away their intellectual property.

But it's not just China, Staynings explains. Even so, because they don't hide what they are doing, China provides easy examples of the kind of risks that organizations in the West are facing.

"All of the BRICS nations have some form of corruption, but India and Brazil are not quite as entrenched as Russia and China," Staynings offers. "In China, they aren't even bothering to mask their IP addresses. They have no compunction about planting interns studying at a local university. Chinese students who, to Western eyes, look like undergraduates could easily be in their late twenties with PhDs in pharmacology. We found pinhole cameras hidden in the ceiling tiles above the PCs. They were recording all the finger movements of all the researchers who were entering data into the system so they could reverse-engineer it."

What is the alternative, when it comes to the potential risks and benefits of working with China or organizational partners from other emerging economies? It's really hard to answer that question. Adding cultural competence and respect to the mix works out well when it comes to most globally oriented organizational strategies. Not being culturally competent and respectful is as problematic as giving away intellectual property. Leaders need to be aware of the risk, or, on some level, they may have to admit that doing business with China isn't worth it.

In trying to be culturally competent and respectful, companies literally give away their intellectual property.

This desire for data is just as critical for leaders to understand as the threat of ransomware. Even without the need for immediate financial gain, the risks are high.

WHEN IT COMES TO risk management, leaders have to invest where it counts.

The CIA triad of priorities—namely confidentiality, integrity, and availability—need to be your focal point when it comes to managing risk. Confidentiality is a set of high-level rules that limits access to all types of data and information. Integrity is the assurance that the information is trustworthy and accurate. And availability is a form of risk management to guarantee reliable access to that information by authorized people.

But even the CIA priorities have their limits.

Jon Washburn, CISO at the law firm Stoel Rives, brings more than thirty years of information technology, security, and governance experience to bear.

People in health care often think "that if you look at confidentiality, integrity, and availability, the three pillars, number one is confidentiality when it comes to health care organizations," Washburn explains. "But it's not confidentiality. I relate it to the idea of having surgery and needing a blood transfusion. Integrity means that, when I receive that blood transfusion, it's the right blood type. Availability is the next most important thing: if that blood is miles away, it's not going to help me survive. Confidentiality is the idea that it's important to protect knowledge about my blood type from getting out there. When you're on the operating room table, it hardly matters."

On the flip side, Washburn explains that confidentiality is of the utmost importance for legal firms. It's number one, integrity is number two, and availability is number three.

"And if you look at manufacturing," Washburn goes on to say, "number one is a toss-up between availability and integrity depending on what you're building."

Washburn is correct. Everything depends on your industry and your strategy.

And Staynings agrees.

"The health care industry, because of its regulatory focus, tends to be overly focused on confidentiality, but this should not come at the expense of cybersecurity. The HIPAA Security Rule of 1996 was written before cybersecurity was an issue. But perhaps even more relevant is the fact that 73 percent of American medical records have already been disclosed and are freely available on the Russian dark web for anyone who wants to buy them. Even more so, kids today put everything about themselves on social media, and they don't have the same privacy expectations as baby boomers. In fact, they build online identities around the medical conditions."

Determine the most important confidentiality, integrity, and availability-of-information assets and systems in your organization. This will help you to identify the right frameworks for determining the likelihood and potential impact of one of these threats on the information being protected.

"People really undervalue understanding the threat landscape," warns Kevin O'Connor. He should know, based on his life experiences. In middle school, he was caught "hacking" computers. Instead of punishment, his teachers enrolled him in an elite computer syllabus, which was the first milestone leading to a career as a threat researcher with the NSA. Based on years of studying the enemy and responding to nation-state attacks, he recommends that organizations prioritize risk management spending by the nature of their business. "It's really about understanding the threat landscape, where you fit in, what you're trying to protect, and your obligations."

Ensure that risk management is a measurable priority for your organization. Adopting an established framework such as the National Institute of Standards and Technology Risk

Management Framework, Committee of Sponsoring Organizations' Enterprise Risk Management, or the ISO 31000 standard is a great place to start that conversation, but it needs to go further than that. You should be creating a risk management plan with your legal counsel and accountants that aligns with your specific business risks.

Maintain a risk register and revisit risk treatments on a regular basis. This is an ongoing task that should not just take place once a year. Ensure your organization is mitigating risk to an acceptable level. This also ought to include deciding where you can eliminate wasteful operations that give your organization a false sense of confidence. Lean into a continuous risk management process that helps identify reasonably foreseeable internal and external threats.

Develop reasonable policies and procedures and adequate technical controls to address these risks. Work with your whole organizational team to look at how to deploy risk management at all levels. For example, Staynings suggests small security changes like buying reflective screens that can't be photographed in intellectually oriented organizations, or hard-wiring keyboards into motherboards, rather than using USB keys, to prevent physical access. Invest in understanding and managing risks that are central to your core organizational needs, rather than following general guidelines.

PART FOUR

THE FUTURE OF CYBERCRIME

12

EMBRACING AI

ET'S PRETEND you're driving in a car on a busy highway. I'm not specifically talking about a car with automatic driving features, but rather any late-model automobile that has built-in sensors that alert you when you're close to the car beside you with a gentle beep and a few tiny flashing lights on your side mirror.

All of a sudden, you crash into the car beside you. The system didn't work. You hear another crash behind you, and you see a Tesla ram into a median. Within seconds, every car on the road is a wreck and people are trying to escape their vehicles.

Why is this happening?

Because instead of recognizing other objects on the road as solids, car computing systems suddenly interpreted them as liquids, like rain. This could happen if the car's communication system, usually equipped with Bluetooth, was infiltrated with adversarial AI commands.

Adversarial machine learning, a technique that attempts to fool AI models with deceptive data, is a growing threat in AI and machine learning and in cybersecurity. An adversarial attack generates examples within AI that are purposely designed to cause a model to make a mistake in its predictions, like in the highway example above.

AI can poison the data lake.

Technically, the use of AI means that it would be unequivocally simple to inform every computer in a network that all cars were made of cake or all dogs were carrying dangerous bombs. It would be just as easy to change the message on every electronic road sign within a network or tell airline systems that all planes are missing. This can happen in many different ways. A whitebox attack, for example, is a scenario where the attacker has complete access to an AI model, including the model's architecture and its parameters, but a blackbox attack can take place where an attacker has no access to the model at all. It's simply a matter of finding a means to feed new data and examples into that system.

Today's deep-learning AI systems can teach themselves to perform certain tasks, from pattern recognition to translation to production, by mimicking the layers of neurons in a human brain and crunching vast amounts of data. Organizations, whether designed for profit or for serving human needs, are now having to operate in the boundless economy of time and space in worldwide situations that are constantly linked to information.

Something that I'm observing about AI in organizations is that attitudes about it are binary. Too binary.

There are organizations throwing the baby out with the bathwater and eschewing AI altogether. These are the leaders who are highly cynical, believing that AI is Skynet from the Terminator franchise, terrified of it taking over the world because they think it will be abused, and advocating for fear-mongering tactics.

Then there are the organizations that are adopting it and not thinking about the possible consequences on their security.

They see the adoption of AI as a cost savings, thinking it's going to accelerate whatever present abilities they have. But, as Jon Washburn advises, that's a big problem. "Every time organizations move up one incremental or logarithmic level in complexity, there are fewer and fewer people who understand it and can figure out if it's been manipulated," he says.

Either way, most leaders' ideas about AI are based on emotion, not logic. There isn't enough research taking place. They're not doing their due diligence to truly determine whether AI is going to work and whether they can protect themselves from the risks that come with it.

As you've probably surmised by now, AI can be bad for humanity and for organizations. It can also be good for humanity and for organizations. It all depends on what we decide to do with it.

JUST LIKE moving into the internet age, moving into the AI age is bound to offer some shortcuts that work to protect us. As much as AI presents an opportunity for cyberwarriors, it can also help us to create new ways of blocking attacks. In cybersecurity, the shift to AI has generated a new way of thinking about the work that we do and why we do it. In this new space, what is absolutely true is that the more tools and ideas that we have that AI generates, the more we will begin to use these tools to do some of the work of keeping organizations safe.

Robert Johnston suggests that organizations can use the same garbage data poison as cybercriminals to defend their own data, misleading hackers. He also suggests that AI can enhance penetration testing support by creating algorithms that reinforce the gates.

"AI is definitely a net positive," he says. "It makes information consumption faster, which is great for data science. Cybersecurity is one of those domains with huge amounts of quickly moving information. Because it is impossible for a human to make sense of that much information, AI presents a perfect use case. A big problem in cybersecurity used to be the fact that scaling up had to be performed by people. The rise of analytics and AI allows us to break that model and alleviate a massive labor shortage in security."

He's not wrong about that labor shortage in IT. Research findings demonstrate that IT professionals are dissatisfied in their job roles on a globally broad scale and that they have inured themselves to the expectation of high stress, long hours, and poor work-life balance to the point at which attrition is through the roof.[1] IT professionals are likely to leave for organizations that provide them with more money, and they switch jobs frequently.

But it's equally important to recognize that we still need IT professionals to make decisions that work for organizations.

"It's ghastly, this gaslighting of the leadership layer over AI," Washburn says. "Leaders are talking about AI as if it's the Holy Grail. But if it's not that, it's something else. Every eighteen months, there's something new, and everybody jumps on the bandwagon. What we really need in organizations is defensive depth. Leaders have to beware of the constant con, the way that they are subjected to the selling of new ideas."

How can we figure out what's going to work and what isn't? Both Washburn and Johnston come back to leader IQ.

"There is a big difference between substantive understanding and mechanical understanding," Washburn offers. "Think about a technology like a spellchecker," he goes on to say. "When that came along, you probably noticed some problems in its spelling recommendations. But you were able to notice when and how you should change your document to make it correct because you have a substantive understanding of spelling honed over the course of your lifetime. But as you get into AI content generation, spellcheck is the least of your worries.

Build your AI knowledge arsenal before waiting for the enemy to one-up you and your business.

You won't have the universal knowledge to understand whether the content created by the AI is valuable. And, if you ask too many questions, you might hit a wall where it not only can't help you, but it might hinder your organization in an active way because you're limited to a mechanical understanding of the content you've created. It's worse than the telephone game."

And as Washburn says, this doesn't mean that you have to throw out AI. But leaders have to be clear about that gap between their own substantive understanding and mechanical understanding.

We can lament the fact that we've opened Pandora's box. Are we facing a technological tectonic shift much like the calculator or spellchecker? Or is this the dawn of our own demise, as foretold in the 2004 to 2009 sci-fi TV series *Battlestar Galactica*, in which Cylons, human-invented AI, turn against their masters and force the survivors of humanity to find another home in the galaxy? Either way, all this has happened before, and all this will happen again.[2]

LEARNING HOW AI applies to your field of battle and how to have productive conversations around the future of cybercrime is imperative for your organization. Build your AI knowledge arsenal before waiting for the enemy to one-up you and your business.

Figure out what data you have that might be targeted and poisoned. Your systems are only as good as the data you've trained them on. Get your tagging clear and rely on data scientists to define your system parameters.

Understand your AI content risks. With AI, anyone might create a fake legal brief or use fake case law. We're already seeing this happen, even within companies themselves, when employees are under pressure to perform and take shortcuts. Find out if there are parts of your business that could be at risk from the use of generative AI.

Prevent the risk of data disclosure to AI systems. If you have proprietary data processes and content, make sure it's codified into data groups that include extra security layers. Don't leave it all in one place.

Ensure that the AI doesn't hallucinate. Your AI systems can pull information from discrete, curated data sets so that they cannot grossly misinterpret your organizational aims.

13

CHOOSING
TO LEAD

BUSINESS LEADERS have made predictions based on their best knowledge of their industries, companies, and technologies, but many of their predictions simply haven't happened.

We've missed amping up ideas like blockchain, and we've overemphasized technologies like drones and virtual reality, assuming they were going to be everywhere in the business world by now, for example. It's possible that business leaders changed their minds on these technologies during a critical time period. Or the technologies themselves changed, or competition entered the market that didn't exist before. Or their teams learned what was working and what wasn't while they were doing their development, and their consumer bases and their boards reacted either positively or negatively to their choices, and then they changed again.

The point is that, despite millions if not billions of dollars, time, and people invested in these decisions, the sidelining of groundbreaking and disruptive ideas happens all the time because we don't always get things right.

We used to think that those who managed organizations the best were those who relied on their unconscious reactions, what most of us would call a "gut instinct." It's almost a leadership trope, the idea of that lone visionary who simply intuited what would make money and followed their idea to the bank. The reality, though, is that after decades of testing, researchers have found that following our gut instincts actually puts us at a massive disadvantage: in doing so, we choose the wrong job paths, unhealthy foods, and even poor relationships.[1]

The people who achieve more of their goals, the same research has shown, are those who take a bit more of a circuitous path to making a decision. This doesn't mean that they spend a whole lot more time making that decision, but that they have better tools, such as self-awareness, reflection, and adaptability—all skills that are essential in succeeding today and into the future.

Think about the choice to run a yellow light. There are probably several dozen considerations at stake in the car and in the physical space around your car. Is it an empty rural road or an urban environment? Is it a matter of conventionally turning left on a yellow in the midst of traffic? Hitting the intersection just as the green turned yellow, or rushing to get to the line just as it turns red? Do you just really want to run the light for some reason you've justified to yourself? Chances are, no matter what the variables, on a yellow light, you make a split decision that doesn't register unless something goes wrong that changes the rest of your day.

Researchers tell us that these kinds of split decisions don't always register with us for a reason. Our brains have, quite literally, the ability to drive our cars even when we're not aware of doing it. We all have a set of brain structures called the default mode network, and it's something that even newborns have. A series of studies at the universities of Cambridge and York in the United Kingdom have shown that once we learn how to do something, such as playing a game or driving a car, our brains allow us to do those tasks without thinking about them consciously.[2]

In fact, when we act in default mode more often (and we can actually learn how to train our own default mode), the same research shows that we can make better choices in general, rather than just for the subconscious decisions connected to typical default-mode activities. In fact, self-awareness plays a role in managing the balance between default and conscious decisions to our advantage.[3] The default mode's role in self-awareness, or, in practical terms, reflection on what we do and what matters to us, makes it useful in consolidating and using our memories.

Why is all of this important to leadership? Why is this important to cybersecurity?

This information is critical. Our self-aware intuition, as defined by social psychologists, is based on large numbers of patterns gained through experience, resulting in different forms of underlying knowledge, knowledge that we don't think about all of the time.[4] This new definition of intuition suggests that experts need to acquire thousands of patterns to actually become experts. I'm not talking about that 10,000-hour guess-timate of spending time repeating a task; I'm talking about practicing thousands of different ways of doing your job based on new inputs.

It's kind of like a marathon runner choosing a new location for each mile of practice, or, in cybersecurity terms, like an IT expert exposed to twenty-odd years of security breaches. Accumulating knowledge from these patterns isn't about mastering generic tools. It's about taking the time to practice and ruminate on direct and vicarious experiences.

Choosing to lead is about stripping away your ego in the service of something bigger.

As a leader, I want you to think about whether you have the kinds of experiences that result in accurate and comprehensive knowledge about cybersecurity. Reading this book doesn't count. Sure, it's made you more aware, but there is more to security than awareness. Think about who you know on your team who already has this kind of expertise, ready to go, within the default mode network in their brain. Is that person you?

Let's get real. Unless you cut your teeth in IT, it's not you.

AS I MENTIONED at the beginning of this book, you can face the future of digital invasions as a victim, or you can face the future as a leader.

Choosing to lead is about stripping away your ego in the service of something bigger. Leaders recognize that they have to surround themselves with the best. Leaders recognize that they have to cede their own ideas to those who have better knowledge and experience. Leaders recognize that they are responsible for all of their stakeholders' needs.

The reason I'm emphasizing these ideas is because the single biggest barrier to cybersecurity, in my experience, is those leaders who fail to listen to their IT teams. When it comes to cybersecurity, there could not be any bigger risk for your organization.

Being a leader in the age of cyberwarfare means honing your security skills, but it also means checking in with your leadership skills. If you're going to secure your gates against those who want you to fail, pay out, or literally stop existing as an organization, it will become fundamental to your role to level up your leadership abilities. That's why building self- and other-awareness will become necessary for developing your IQ over the years to come.

Think about the average company for a moment. A company is designed, fundamentally, to fulfill a mission or goal. People are assigned roles to take part in that fulfillment process. That company also defines its values and the outcomes it wants to achieve in each year of its strategic plan so that it is easier to match people with those roles. However, most of us slip into those roles as if they were character assignments. We create our own personal brands on LinkedIn or on our company websites in order to fit in perfectly with the keywords recruiters are targeting. Social economists call this a company's embeddedness: the social context that governs everything a company does has definitions, keywords, character expectations, and rote experiences. Organizations have these defining characteristics, and, as a result, people are bound by these specific social roles.

This is especially the case in cybersecurity events.

In my work, I've found that there are a number of personalities who make up the ranks during a cybersecurity event. While not directly mapped to personality models or types, the following cast of characters often appears during cyber incidents. Each character brings assets and liabilities to the table. Think of each character as the light and shadow of a persona or archetype.

The hero. This individual comes from all ranks of the business and exhibits a strongly proactive desire to make decisions and take immediate action, succumbing to their fight-or-flight instincts. This character is driven by ego, often acts as a lone wolf, and will go as far as to counter group directions. Actions are often unilateral and presented to enhance personal achievement in front of senior executives or stakeholders. When actions align with business interests and incident specifics, results are positive, whereas misaligned actions can result in negative consequences. Consider the 2017 ransomware attack on the prominent law firm DLA Piper. A middle-ranked IT employee posted unauthorized public warnings exposing the incident and created a public relations disaster for the firm.[5]

The martyr. This individual feels responsible for either the cause or response to the incident and works tirelessly to contain the attack. They feel compelled to remain at work, volunteer for tasks, and refuse to take personal breaks. This character becomes fatigued, operates from fear of professional loss or termination, and is susceptible to mistakes and errors caused by exhaustion. They often rush decisions and actions to rectify issues and can miss critical details in haste. Rapid actions often cause second-order consequences such as public outages or service disruptions when critical systems are disabled to stop the lateral spread of malware or adversarial movement.

The hinderer. This individual exemplifies passive-aggressive behaviors, avoiding group conflict in preference for individual heroic actions. This individual "knows best" and acts in the self-declared interest of their firm. They often remain passive or in implied agreement with the group, but they wait for one-to-one opportunities to influence or sway decision-makers into reversing group decisions. Their actions appear subversive and can divide the group and erode trust.

The hoarder. This individual hoards information in an attempt to achieve power status in the group, influence decision-makers, and appear more informed and intelligent than their peers. Like hinderers, their actions convey a subversive agenda and can divide the group or erode trust. Moreover, withholding critical information hinders the ability of the group to make informed decisions and can lead to easily avoided negative consequences.

The captain. This individual sees the world through the lens of rank and seniority and establishes dominance over the group as the highest-ranking member. Their word goes, and they dismiss decision-making challenges. In some cases, seniority is assumed based on company ownership or professional role (lawyer or doctor) and not on expertise related to cyber incidents. They can ignore critical information or recommendations delivered by those they perceive as subordinate or inferior. They also foster a military-like culture in which subordinates assume the leader is correct and carry out their orders without question. An extreme example of this dynamic played out the cockpit of Korean Air Flight 801, as the co-pilot and flight engineer deferred to the captain on final approach into Guam and failed to inform the captain of critical errors, leading to a crash into the side of a mountain and killing 229 of the 254 souls on board. The 1997 accident and subsequent investigation led to major crew changes at the airline, intentionally dismantling the hierarchical, military style of leadership and empowering subordinates to challenge the orders and actions of senior flight crew.[6]

The lawyer. The layperson lawyer lacks any actual qualifications but has synergized assumption and pseudo-expertise from various online sources, popular media, and second-hand experience in cyber incidents. They are quick to examine facts and decisions through a lens of litigation and make recommendations based on perceived legal jeopardy, including customer notifications of breaches, internal employee communications, technical actions, and law enforcement notifications. The lawyer provides guidance that is anywhere from completely inaccurate, to lacking granularity or contextual relevance, to correct.

Cyber incidents are stressful, with significant business risk in terms of reputation, financial and professional losses, and operational resilience. If we play into these roles, this cast of characters is not going to help us make decisions fast enough and proficiently enough.

Unfortunately, once we slip into these character roles, they can be difficult to shift.

Actors are paid to play characters. The reason actors can play people who have different life paths is because the sets of rules we live by, even outside of the office, are so defined. Writers can give them lines so they say the right things to become a hockey player, a single mother, a CEO. Put a cowboy hat on them and an actor is a cowboy. These roles are, in writing parlance, called tropes, and they're used over and over again by screenwriters on purpose because we actually deeply enjoy seeing something we can recognize on the screen, even if it's the same every time.

That's why we do the same thing at work. We become who we *think* we should be based on stereotypes, not on who we ought to be to lead our organizations.

LEADERS HAVE TO step away from being stereotypes.

The role of leader, just like the other roles I've mentioned here, is also tied to a set of unwritten but highly specific social rules that we learn to adhere to unconsciously. Self-awareness in leadership requires conscious commitment to see what's in our blind spots, to see what we haven't seen before.

Being aware doesn't mean you're always going to be wrong when you're sparring with your CISO or that your gut feeling is going to lead you in the wrong direction. But you can begin to be reflective and honest about where you're usually right, where you're probably right, and where you know that you need more information from the people on your team to make a decision that works.

Where are you right now in terms of your actual expertise regarding the security of your unique organization? Where do you want to be?

What's the first thing you can do to get to the root of the problem?

What can you trust about what you know, and what can't you trust yet?

What might you need to push yourself on to find out the next step in the process for you?

Leaders need to embrace polarizing points of view. When we're building an organization that is going to succeed in the wake of imminent danger, we can't simply create new networks of sameness. The people we want in our organizations are those who challenge us. If the people in our organizations are distinct and unique enough, our organizations will also become distinct and unique, and they will be able to adapt to danger.

That's why, when it comes to cybersecurity, the role of leaders is only going to become more critical in the years to come. Allowing ourselves to question what we know and build on real-life practices accelerates the process. We create our own personal learning strategies when we have agency to be authentic.[7] This happens through finding meaning in our work (through learning as experience); community (through mutual engagement, joint enterprise, and shared repertoire); identity (through learning and use of shared resources); and practice (through shared goals and learning as doing). Leadership isn't about being the best at something; it is about learning how to adapt to the myriad changes we will constantly face in every aspect of our existence, every moment we are alive, and sharing that experience with a team.

The world will continue to move faster than it does today, and much faster than it did a decade ago. As a result, we have to recognize that since the world is changing faster and faster, we have to as well. All of this requires a new framework, a new way of setting our bearings repeatedly, so we can assess and reassess and, above all, feel *good* about our future.

Our societal ability to look past the dark challenges we've been leaning into and, instead, look for possibility and potential depends on you.

14

ENDGAME

THE ONE CONSTANT in cybersecurity is change. Adversaries have first-mover advantage in terms of technical and tactical advancement. It's an arms race that takes no prisoners.

The hunt for a magic bullet will leave you empty handed. While it's reasonable to expect salvation from those whose job it is to protect us, that help won't come anytime soon. As an FBI agent once said to me, the cavalry isn't riding over the hill. His advice: strap on your proverbial six-shooter and be prepared to defend your own homestead. Law enforcement is under-resourced and overwhelmed. We've seen some progress with arrests and takedowns of leak sites and malware-sharing depots. Yet, another adversary debuts or a new leak site is live days later.

Some people liken stopping cybercrime to the Whac-A-Mole game. To me, it's on the scale of the magically replicating cups in Bellatrix Lestrange's Gringotts bank vault, in the Harry Potter universe. Or it's a multiheaded hydra of Greek mythology that grows back when decapitated. Pick your metaphor. They each sum it up some days when I think about stemming the flow of stolen money.

While governments have entered the fray, it seems even massive resources cannot stop this form of war. The enemy knows it, too. As we've seen repeated through history, smaller forces employing guerrilla tactics and using the terrain to their advantage can hold superior forces at bay for years, if not decades. Take Afghanistan, for example. Centuries of conflict have scarred the land and shaped the people. Only the color of the occupying military's uniforms provides a clue as to what decade it is.

VUCA says positive change is not going to happen. The Dark Future scale says it's unlikely.

Even though the potential for risk elevation seems endless, we can still have hope. It's hope of a whole different caliber.

I have hope in people. People persevere no matter the strife or horrific circumstances. Life finds a way. Most of all, I have hope in leaders. Unlike technology, good leaders can adapt to new information and new circumstances. Leaders are not binary. We're fixated on artificial intelligence that can learn and adapt. Perhaps we should put at least the same effort into our human capital.

This is an opportune time to create new standards for leadership, standards that will not only improve our job and organizational skills but also perhaps make us better people in the process. An organizational approach to success that thrives on confidentiality, integrity, and availability is one worth developing. Here are a few recommendations to start this change:

- **Confidence.** Leaders have to get comfortable in making changes that support cybersecurity best practices. They have to get comfortable talking about why confidentiality, integrity, and availability are needed, with the personal confidence and skill to share their leadership development process with other members of the team without hesitation.

You have what it takes to lead, and now you know what it's going to take to lead in a crisis.

Leaders can seek out and validate opinions aligned with the best interests of all stakeholders and integrate these into their own models for change.

- **Culture acceleration.** Leaders who succeed are really clear on roles and responsibilities, as well as functionality in roles and teams. A culture of collaboration is built from the inside and ripples outward through the creation of rich relationships. This requires a focus on building authentic trust and accelerating inclusion so that everyone can take on an empowered role to keep the organization safe.

- **Connection.** Building links between cybersecurity and the needs of people, both inside and outside an organization, has an amplification effect on organizational safety and risk management. An integrated approach that draws a line between ideals and goals, connecting all of the dots, is needed.

Whenever you learn a new skill at work, you adopt it at the pace of what's called the learning curve. It's slow at the beginning, no matter what field we are in. New research suggests that the learning curve can no longer be described in terms of sequential development that eventually leads to mastery, nor as something that can be achieved within the confines of a training program or workload.[1] Self-beliefs and perceptions affect how the learning curve progresses: stresses, burnout, and imposter syndrome all factor into whether this curve progresses at its normal upward rate. Our insecurity is associated with decreases in our ability to absorb new information.

But we can get unstuck. We can lead our organizations into new ways of thinking and doing. Allowing ourselves to question what we know and build on real-life examples of what can go wrong (and right) in terms of cybersecurity, just as we've achieved in this book, is going to accelerate the process.

You have what it takes to lead, and now you know what it's going to take to lead in a crisis.

The future includes an inclusive and participatory decision-making practice that draws from the knowledge and experience of multiple stakeholders, especially those within your organization. This has to start now. It can't start when the ransom is on the table. The future requires your self-awareness, empathy, integrity, and a commitment to personal and collective growth. This happens through finding meaning in your work (through learning as experience); community (through mutual engagement, joint enterprise, and shared repertoire); identity (through learning and use of shared resources); and practice (through shared goals and learning as doing). The future needs an integration of organizational trust, transparency, collaboration, and IQ building congruent with new global priorities. We need to support people who are aware of what they have and what we can all do right now in order to actualize our futures. Our work communities need to change direction from a power-based orientation to governance structures that allow for trust-building and collaboration.

Cybercrime isn't going away anytime soon. Assuming it will is as futile as thinking you can control the weather to suit your whims. Ship captains know better. They gauge the weather, keep an eye on the forecast, and know they cannot command the sea. In other words, they are conscious of what they can control and what they can't. They know when to defer to mother nature. In our VUCA world, consider the same approach in more generalized terms: know what's right, know what matters, and know what's yours.

ACKNOWLEDGMENTS

WISH TO THANK Tim Evans and Robert Johnston for supporting this project, offering me the chance to continue my research, and entertaining my off-the-beaten-path approach to cybersecurity. I commend Steve Mai and Michelle Sangster for their willingness to tell their stories. I wish to highlight the accomplishments of Deborah Snyder, Tracy Wareing Evans, and Lisa Plaggemier for their leadership in public service and cybersecurity. Richard Staynings, Jon Washburn, and John Caruthers are cyberveterans who have by far given more to their respective communities than they have likely received back.

I wish to acknowledge new friends and colleagues like Miguel Hablutzel, Kevin O'Connor, James Lin, Kirsten Bay, Stefan Korshak, Harrison Green-Fishback, and Kara Wayman for their respective contributions.

And I wish to thank Kristen Farnum and Bob Darling for their kindness, humble expertise, and service to their country.

Lastly, I wish to thank Vince Molinaro, a fellow Page Two author, for helping me take that first step toward writing a book. While he taught me the ins and outs of publishing, he also gave me a new frame of reference, helping me realize that writing a book was not an unsurmountable project.

NOTES

Introduction

1   Catherine Roberts, "The Privacy Problems of Direct-to-Consumer Genetic Testing," *Consumer Reports*, January 11, 2022, consumerreports.org/health/dna-test-kits/privacy-and-direct -to-consumer-genetic-testing-dna-test-kits-a1187212155/.

2   UK Information Commissioner's Office, "ICO to Investigate 23andMe Data Breach with Canadian Counterpart," June 10, 2024, ico.org.uk/about-the-ico/media-centre/news-and-blogs/ 2024/06/ico-to-investigate-23andme-data-breach-with -canadian-counterpart.

3   US Government Accountability Office, "The U.S. Is Less Prepared to Fight Cybercrime Than It Could Be," GAO's *WatchBlog*, August 29, 2023, gao.gov/blog/u.s.-less-prepared-fight -cybercrime-it-could-be.

Chapter 1: Infiltration Is a Given

1   Sophos, *The State of Ransomware 2024*, whitepaper, April 2024, sophos.com/en-us/content/state-of-ransomware.

2   Adlumin, *Adversary Trends and Recent Vulnerabilities*, Volume I, 2024, adlumin.com/resource/adlumins-threat-insights-2024 -volume-i.

3   US Department of the Treasury, "Treasury Takes Robust Actions to Counter Ransomware," September 21, 2021, home.treasury .gov/news/press-releases/jy0364.

4   Alessandro Lanteri, "Strategic Drivers for the Fourth Industrial Revolution," *Thunderbird International Business Review* 63, no. 3 (2021): 273–83, doi.org/10.1002/tie.22196.

5 US Centers for Disease Control and Prevention, "Lightning Strike Victim Data," April 15, 2024, cdc.gov/lightning/data-research/index.html.

6 Kalle Radage, "The Number of Businesses in the USA and Statistics for 2024," Clearly Payments, May 24, 2024, clearlypayments.com/blog/the-number-of-businesses-in -the-usa-and-statistics-for-2024.

7 SentinelOne, "Key Cyber Security Statistics for 2024," September 12, 2024, sentinelone.com/cybersecurity-101/ cybersecurity/cyber-security-statistics/.

Chapter 2: Evolving Battle Tactics

1 Dan Goodin, "Chinese Malware Removed from SOHO Routers After FBI Issues Covert Commands," *Ars Technica*, January 31, 2024, arstechnica.com/security/2024/01/chinese-malware -removed-from-soho-routers-after-fbi-issues-covert-commands/2.

2 Europol, "International Collaboration Leads to Dismantlement of Ransomware Group in Ukraine Amidst Ongoing War," updated November 28, 2023, europol.europa.eu/media-press/newsroom/ news/international-collaboration-leads-to-dismantlement-of -ransomware-group-in-ukraine-amidst-ongoing-war.

3 "Russia Is Ramping Up Sabotage Across Europe," *The Economist*, May 12, 2024, economist.com/europe/2024/05/12/russia-is -ramping-up-sabotage-across-europe.

4 Office of Foreign Assets Control, "Mission," US Department of the Treasury, n.d., ofac.treasury.gov.

Chapter 3: Building Risk Awareness

1 Bob Johansen, *Get There Early: Sensing the Future to Compete in the Present* (Berrett-Koehler, 2007).

Chapter 4: Respecting the Technology Baseline

1 Akshay Kulkarni, "State Actor Blamed for Cyberattack on BC Government Systems," CBC News, May 10, 2024, cbc.ca/news/ canada/british-columbia/bc-government-cyberattack-state -actor-1.7200735.

2 Arun Sukumar, Dennis Broeders, and Monica Kello, "The Pervasive Informality of the International Cybersecurity Regime: Geopolitics, Non-state Actors, and Diplomacy," *Contemporary*

Security Policy 45, no. 1 (2024): 7–44, doi.org/10.1080/13523260.20
23.2296739.

3   Nir Hassid and Eviatar Matania, "A Global Regime for Cybersecurity and the Obstacles to Future Progress," *Global
Governance: A Review of Multilateralism and International
Organizations* 30, no. 1 (2024): 13–40, ssrn.com/abstract=
4842370.

4   Ramses A. Wessel and Tatiana Nascimento Heim, "The Various
Dimensions of Cyberthreats: (In)consistencies in the Global
Regulation of Cybersecurity," *Anales de Derecho* 40 (2023):
40–65, doi.org/10.6018/analesderecho.546921.

5   Communications Security Establishment Canada, "Canada Joins
International Security Partners in Release of Advisory, Guidance
on Growing Cyber Security Threat to Civil Society," Government
of Canada, May 14, 2024, canada.ca/en/communications-security/
news/2024/05/canada-joins-international-security-partners-in
-release-of-advisory-guidance-on-growing-cyber-security-threat
-to-civil-society.html.

6   Catherine Tunney, "Canadian Agencies Do Not Have the Capacity
or Capability to Police Cybercrime: AG," CBC News, June 4, 2024,
cbc.ca/news/politics/cyber-crime-rcmp-ag-1.7223887.

7   National Criminal Justice Information and Statistics Service,
Computer Crime: Criminal Justice Resource Manual, US
Department of Justice, 1979, 3, ojp.gov/ncjrs/virtual-library/
abstracts/computer-crime-criminal-justice-resource-manual.

8   Internet Crime Complaint Center (IC3), *2023 Internet Crime
Report*, Federal Bureau of Investigation, 2024, ic3.gov/Annual
Report/Reports/2023_IC3Report.pdf.

9   Xiaotong He, "The Impact of Russia-Ukraine Cyberwarfare on
the Application of the Right to Self-Defense in Cyberspace and
Implications," *US-China Law Review* 20, no. 3 (2023): 113–25,
dx.doi.org/10.17265/1548-6605/2023.03.003; Mai Trinh Nguyen
and Minh Quang Tran, "Balancing Security and Privacy in
the Digital Age: An In-Depth Analysis of Legal and Regulatory
Frameworks Impacting Cybersecurity Practices," *International
Journal of Intelligent Automation and Computing* 6, no. 5 (2023):
1–12, research.tensorgate.org/index.php/IJIAC/article/view/61;
Arun Sukumar, Dennis Broeders, and Monica Kello, "The
Pervasive Informality of the International Cybersecurity Regime:

Geopolitics, Non-state Actors, and Diplomacy," *Contemporary Security Policy* 45, no. 1 (2024): 7–44, doi.org/10.1080/13523260.20 23.2296739.

10 Tajammul Pangarkar, "Multi-Factor Authentication Statistics 2024 by Best Security," Market.us, updated October 11, 2024, scoop.market.us/multi-factor-authentication-statistics.

Chapter 5: Acknowledging the Disconnect

1 Mark Sangster, *No Safe Harbor: The Inside Truth About Cybercrime—and How to Protect Your Business* (Page Two, 2020).

2 Jeff Kosseff, "Upgrading Cybersecurity Law," *Houston Law Review* 61, no. 1 (2023), dx.doi.org/10.2139/ssrn.4364356.

Chapter 6: Closing Ranks

1 Patrick Lencioni, *Overcoming the Five Dysfunctions of a Team: A Field Guide for Leaders, Managers, and Facilitators* (Jossey-Bass, 2005).

Chapter 7: Understanding That Trust Is a Currency

1 Sicheng Xu et al., "VASA-1: Lifelike Audio-Driven Talking Faces Generated in Real Time," *arXiv* (April 2024), doi.org/10.48550/ arXiv.2404.10667.

2 Christine Lagarde, "There's a Reason for the Lack of Trust in Government and Business: Corruption," *IMFBlog*, May 4, 2018, imf.org/en/Blogs/Articles/2018/05/04/theres-a-reason-for-the -lack-of-trust-in-government-and-business-corruption.

3 Armi Mustosmäki, "The Intensification of Work," in *Family, Work, and Well-Being: Emergence of New Issues*, ed. Mia Tammelin (Springer, 2018), 77–90, doi.org/10.1007/978-3-319-76463-4_7.

4 Gallup, *State of the Global Workplace: 2024*, gallup.com/ workplace/349484/state-of-the-global-workplace.aspx.

5 Jen Fisher et al., "The Important Role of Leaders in Advancing Human Sustainability," Deloitte Insights, June 18, 2024, deloitte.com/us/en/insights/topics/talent/workplace-well-being -research-2024.html.

6 David H. Li (trans.), *The Art of Leadership by Sun Tzu* (Premier, 2001), 28.

7 Simon Linacre, "Time Well Spent? Differing Perceptions of Breaks at Work," *Human Resource Management International Digest* 24, no. 3 (2016): 11–13, dx.doi.org/10.1108/HRMID-02-2016-0020.

8   Rebecca Johannsen and Paul J. Zak, "The Neuroscience of
    Organizational Trust and Business Performance: Findings from
    United States Working Adults and an Intervention at an Online
    Retailer," *Frontiers in Psychology* 11 (2021): 579459, doi.org/
    10.3389/fpsyg.2020.579459.
9   Edward L. Deci and Richard M. Ryan, "The Support of Autonomy
    and the Control of Behavior," *Journal of Personality and Social
    Psychology* 53, no. 6 (1987): 1024–37, doi.org/10.1037/0022-3514
    .53.6.1024.

Chapter 8: Establishing Credibility

1   Dan Goodin, "Chinese Malware Removed from SOHO Routers
    After FBI Issues Covert Commands," *Ars Technica*, January 31,
    2024, arstechnica.com/security/2024/01/chinese-malware
    -removed-from-soho-routers-after-fbi-issues-covert-commands/2.
2   Justin Kruger and David Dunning, "Unskilled and Unaware of It:
    How Difficulties in Recognizing One's Own Incompetence Lead
    to Inflated Self-Assessments," *Journal of Personality and Social
    Psychology* 77, no. 6 (1999): 1121–34, doi.org/10.1037/0022
    -3514.77.6.1121.
3   Jared Diamond, *Collapse: How Societies Choose to Fail or Succeed*
    (Viking, 2005).
4   David A. Spencer, "Fear and Hope in an Age of Mass Automation:
    Debating the Future of Work," *New Technology, Work and
    Employment* 33, no. 1 (2018): 1–12, doi.org/10.1111/ntwe.12105.
5   Peter Newman, Timothy Beatley, and Heather Boyer, *Resilient
    Cities: Overcoming Fossil Fuel Dependence*, 2nd ed. (Island Press,
    2017).
6   Zbigniew Zaleski et al., "Development and Validation of the Dark
    Future Scale," *Time & Society* 28, no. 1 (2019): 107–23, doi.org/
    10.1177/0961463X16678257.
7   Carey K. Morewedge et al., "Debiasing Decisions: Improved
    Decision Making with a Single Training Intervention," *Policy
    Insights from the Behavioral and Brain Sciences* 2, no. 1 (2015):
    129–40, dx.doi.org/10.1177/2372732215600886.
8   Susan Michie, Maartje M. van Stralen, and Robert West, "The
    Behaviour Change Wheel: A New Method for Characterising and
    Designing Behaviour Change Interventions," *Implementation
    Science* 6 (2011): 1–12, doi.org/10.1186/1748-5908-6-42.

Chapter 9: Being Accountable

1   "Cyber Security and Resilience Bill," Department for Science, Innovation and Technology, GOV.UK, September 30, 2024, gov.uk/government/collections/cyber-security-and-resilience-bill.

2   US Securities and Exchange Commission, "SEC Charges SolarWinds and Chief Information Security Officer with Fraud, Internal Control Failures," press release, October 30, 2023, sec.gov/news/press-release/2023-227.

3   Ting Xiang, Terry Lohrenz, and P. Read Montague, "Computational Substrates of Norms and Their Violations During Social Exchange," *Journal of Neuroscience* 33, no. 3 (2013): 1099–108, doi.org/10.1523/JNEUROSCI.1642-12.2013.

4   Wendy Wood and Dennis Rünger, "Psychology of Habit," *Annual Review of Psychology* 67 (2016): 289–314, doi.org/10.1146/annurev-psych-122414-033417.

5   Giuseppe Lorini and Francesco Marrosu, "How Individual Habits Fit/Unfit Social Norms: From the Historical Perspective to a Neurobiological Repositioning of an Unresolved Problem," *Frontiers in Sociology* 3 (2018): 14, doi.org/10.3389/fsoc.2018.00014.

6   Wood and Rünger, "Psychology of Habit."

7   Tara Deschamps, "Indigo Books & Music Shareholders Vote to Approve Privatization Sale," CTV News, May 27, 2024, cheknews.ca/indigo-books-music-shareholders-vote-to-approve-privatization-sale-1206412.

8   Avertium, "MGM/Caesars Post-Mortem and Attribution," September 26, 2023, avertium.com/resources/threat-reports/mgm-caesars-post-mortem-and-attribution.

Chapter 10: Empowering People

1   Jonathan Grieg, "UnitedHealth CEO Confirms Company Paid $22 Million Ransom in Heated Senate Hearing," *The Record*, May 1, 2024, therecord.media/unitedhealth-ceo-testifies-senate-hearing.

2   Milton Friedman, "The Social Responsibility of Business Is to Increase Its Profits," *New York Times Magazine*, September 13, 1970, nytimes.com/1970/09/13/archives/a-friedman-doctrine-the-social-responsibility-of-business-is-to.html.

3   Bess Levin, "Elon Musk, Jeff Bezos, and Warren Buffett Agree: Paying Taxes Is for Poor People," *Vanity Fair*, June 8, 2021, vanityfair.com/news/2021/06/billionaires-federal-income-tax -investigation.

4   Katherine Campbell and Duane Helleloid, "Starbucks: Social Responsibility and Tax Avoidance," *Journal of Accounting Education* 37 (2016): 38–60, doi.org/10.1016/j.jaccedu.2016 .09.001.

5   Sam Jones, "Switzerland Plans Subsidies to Offset G7 Corporate Tax Plan," *Financial Times*, June 9, 2021, ft.com/content/ 8b57bead-4e52-4f07-a2eb-ea46443abfe2.

6   Harvey S. James Jr. and Farhad Rassekh, "Smith, Friedman, and Self-Interest in Ethical Society," *Business Ethics Quarterly* 10, no. 3 (2000): 659–74, doi.org/10.2307/3857897.

7   Anna Medaris, "What Do People Really Want in Their Work? Meaning and Stability," *APA Monitor on Psychology* 55, no. 1 (January/February 2024): 64, apa.org/monitor/2024/01/trends -meaning-stability-workplaces.

Chapter 11: Investing Where It Counts

1   Joby Warrick and Cate Brown, "China's Quest for Human Genetic Data Spurs Fears of a DNA Arms Race," *Washington Post*, September 21, 2023, washingtonpost.com/world/interactive/ 2023/china-dna-sequencing-bgi-covid.

2   Warrick and Brown, "China's Quest for Human Genetic Data Spurs Fears of a DNA Arms Race."

3   Sam Cooper, "Inside the Chinese Military Attack on Nortel," *Global News*, August 25, 2020, globalnews.ca/news/7275588/ inside-the-chinese-military-attack-on-nortel.

4   Jim Duffy, "Cisco Sues Huawei Over Intellectual Property," *Computerworld*, January 23, 2003, computerworld.com/article/ 1335175/cisco-sues-huawei-over-intellectual-property.html.

Chapter 12: Embracing AI

1   Andrea Valéria Steil et al., "Job Satisfaction and Employee Retention by Public and Private IT Organizations," *Revista de Administração da UFSM* 15 (2022): 354–69, doi.org/10.5902/ 1983465968850.

2   While quoted in *Battlestar Galactica*, the original source is Disney's *Peter Pan*.

Chapter 13: Choosing to Lead

1   Mark R. Nieuwenstein et al., "On Making the Right Choice: A Meta-analysis and Large-Scale Replication Attempt of the Unconscious Thought Advantage," *Judgment and Decision Making* 10, no. 1 (2015): 1–17, doi.org/10.1017/S1930297500 003144.

2   Deniz Vatansever, David K. Menon, and Emmanuel A. Stamatakis, "Default Mode Contributions to Automated Information Processing," *Proceedings of the National Academy of Sciences* 114, no. 48 (2017): 12821–26, doi.org/10.1073/pnas.1710521114.

3   Dante Mantini et al., "Default Mode of Brain Function in Monkeys," *Journal of Neuroscience* 31, no. 36 (2011): 12954–62, doi.org/10.1523/JNEUROSCI.2318-11.2011.

4   Alexandre A. Bachkirov, "Managerial Decision Making Under Specific Emotions," *Journal of Managerial Psychology* 30, no. 7 (2015): 861–74, doi.org/10.1108/JMP-02-2013-0071.

5   TitanFile, "DLA Piper Ransomware Hack: What Can We Learn from It?" n.d., titanfile.com/blog/dla-piper-ransomware-hack -can-learn.

6   National Transportation Safety Board, *Aircraft Accident Report: Controlled Flight Into Terrain, Korean Air Flight 801, Boeing 747-300, HL7468, Nimitz Hill, Guam, August 6, 1997* (2000), ntsb.gov/investigations/accidentreports/reports/aar0001.pdf.

7   Etienne Wenger, *Communities of Practice: Learning, Meaning, and Identity* (Cambridge University Press, 1998).

Chapter 14: Endgame

1   Thomas Schipperen, "Linear vs Non-linear Learning and the Future of Work," Lepaya, last updated June 26, 2024, lepaya.com/ blog/linear-and-non-linear-learning.

ABOUT THE AUTHOR

MARK SANGSTER is the author of *No Safe Harbor: The Inside Truth About Cybercrime—and How to Protect Your Business* and *Cyber-Conscious Leadership: A Practical Guide to Protecting Your Organization Against Cybercrime*. He is an award-winning speaker at international conferences and on prestigious stages, including the Harvard Law School and RSA Conference. Mark has appeared on *CNN News Hour* to provide expert opinions on international cybercrime issues and is a go-to subject matter expert for leading publications, including the *Wall Street Journal* and *Forbes*.

Cybersecurity is *not* an IT problem to solve; it's a business risk to manage.

Let's keep the conversation going.

PING ME! I'm always happy to chat, provide some advice, or help with cybersecurity issues.

- **Follow my industry hijinks:** linkedin.com/in/mbsangster

- **Stay in touch for insights and the latest cyber news on Instagram:** @cyber_mbsangster

- **Listen to the latest gossip on *Cybercrime Magazine*'s podcasts:** cybersecurityventures.com/podcasts

- **Visit my website for additional resources, articles, and videos:** mbsangster.com

- **Drop me a line:** mark@mbsangster.com